Disney's

Kim Possible

E 3

Series Created By
Bob Schooley and Mark McCorkle

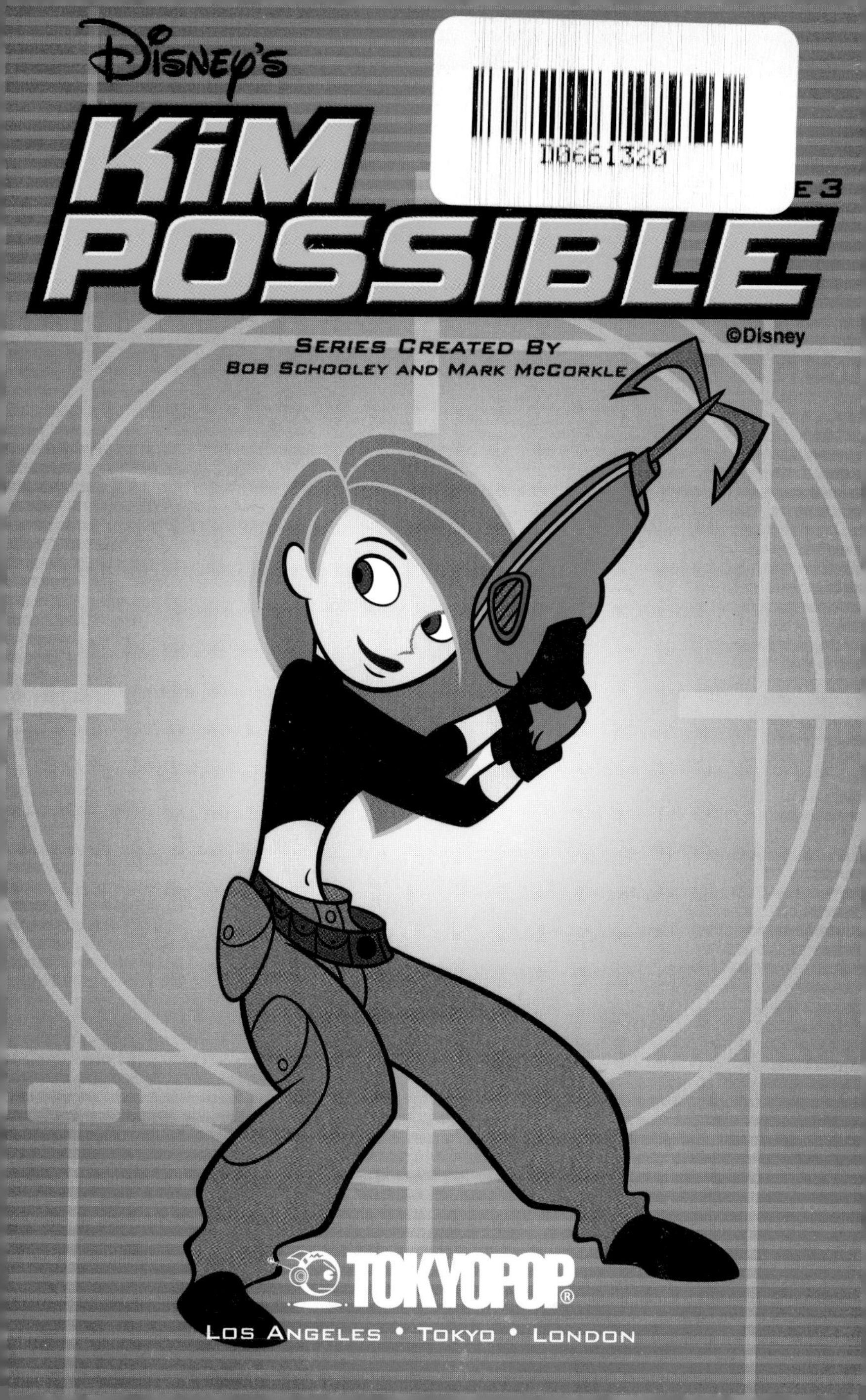

TOKYOPOP®
Los Angeles • Tokyo • London

Contributing Editors - Amy Court Kaemon & Paul Morrissey
Graphic Design & Lettering - Michael Merrill
Graphic Artist - Anna Kernbaum
Cover Layout - Patrick Hook

Editor - Elizabeth Hurchalla
Managing Editor - Jill Freshney
Production Manager - Antonio DePietro
Production Manager - Jennifer Miller
Art Director - Matt Alford
Editorial Director - Jeremy Ross
VP of Production - Ron Klamert
President & C.O.O. - John Parker
Publisher & C.E.O. - Stuart Levy

Email: editor@TOKYOPOP.com
Come visit us online at www.TOKYOPOP.com

A **TOKYOPOP**® Cine-Manga™
TOKYOPOP Inc.
5900 Wilshire Blvd., Suite 2000, Los Angeles, CA 90036

ISBN: 1-59182-243-2

First TOKYOPOP printing: September 2003

10 9 8 7 6 5 4 3 2 1

Printed in Canada

Disney's

KiM POSSIBLE

VOLUME 3

©Disney

CONTENTS:

THE NEW RON....................................6
MIND GAMES....................................50

CHARACTER BIOS

KIM POSSIBLE

A STUDENT AT MIDDLETON HIGH SCHOOL WHO LOVES CHEERLEADING, SHOPPING AND HANGING OUT WITH HER BEST FRIEND RON. BUT KIM'S NO ORDINARY GIRL—SHE CAN DO ANYTHING, INCLUDING SAVING THE WORLD IN HER SPARE TIME.

RON STOPPABLE

KIM'S BEST FRIEND AND SIDEKICK.

RUFUS

RON'S PET NAKED MOLE RAT.

WADE

THE 10-YEAR-OLD GENIUS WHO RUNS KIM'S WEBSITE AND KEEPS HER UPDATED ON EVIL SCHEME DEVELOPMENTS.

KIM'S MOM

A BRAIN SURGEON.

KIM'S DAD

A ROCKET SCIENTIST.

JIM AND TIM POSSIBLE

KIM'S YOUNGER TWIN BROTHERS WHO ARE CONSTANTLY CAUSING KIM DOUBLE TROUBLE.

SEÑOR SENIOR, SENIOR

A MULTIBILLIONAIRE WHO LIVES ON AN UNCHARTED PRIVATE ISLAND.

SEÑOR SENIOR, JUNIOR

SENIOR'S SELF-INVOLVED SON.

DRAKKEN

A BAD GUY WHO WANTS TO TAKE OVER THE WORLD.

SHEGO

DRAKKEN'S GLAMOROUS HENCHGIRL.

PRIVATE CLEOTIS DOBBS

AN ARMY PRIVATE WITH TOP SECURITY CLEARANCE.

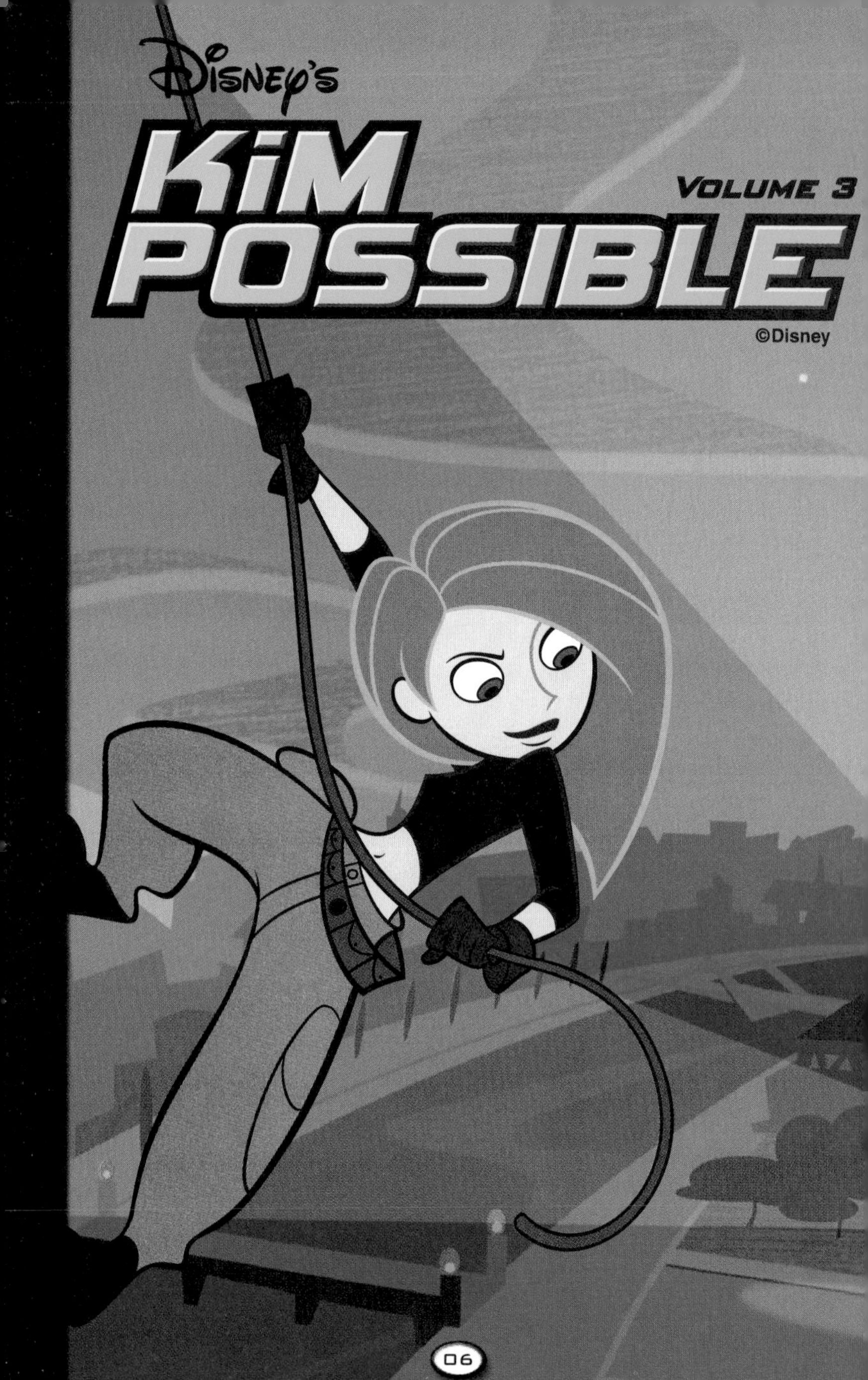
Disney's
Kim Possible
Volume 3
©Disney

EPISODE 5: THE NEW RON

A new haircut gives Ron Stoppable new confidence, not to mention a new, not-so-improved attitude. But when a multibillionaire bad guy and his self-indulgent son threaten to drain Europe of all its electricity, Kim needs all the help she can get. Will she be able to find her old friend in the new Ron?

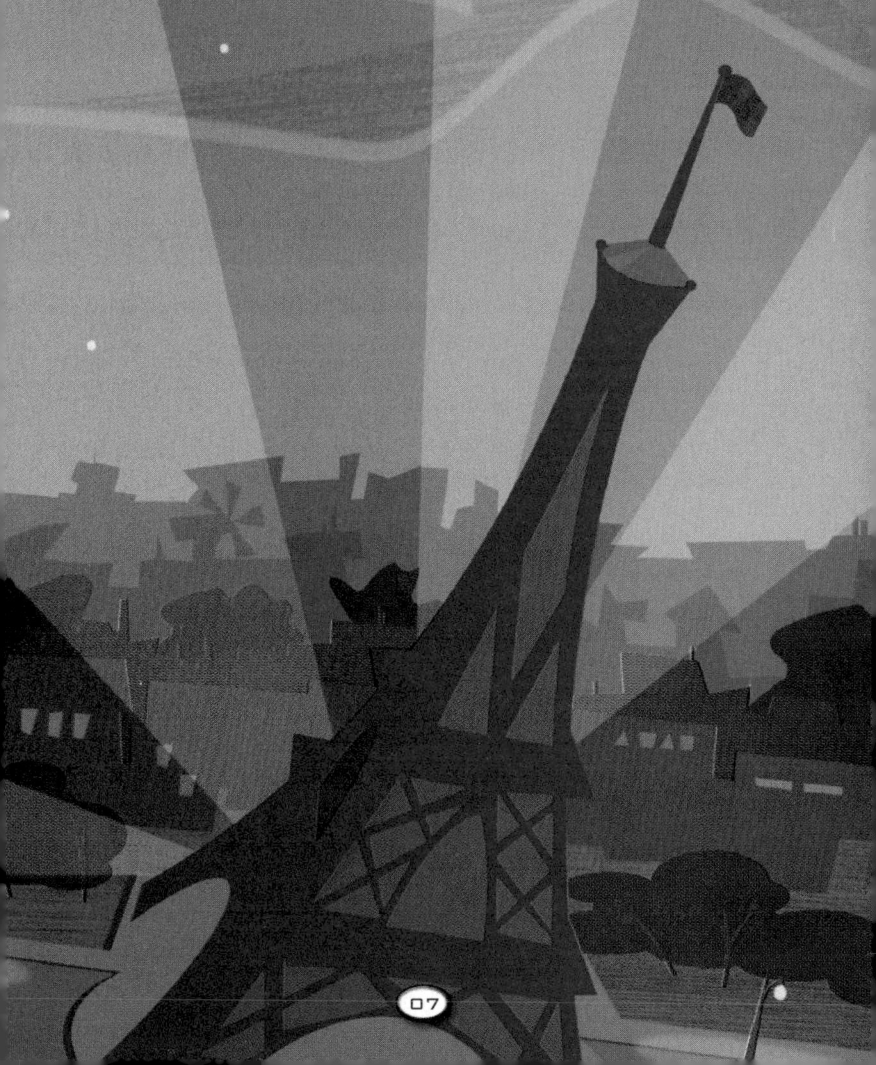

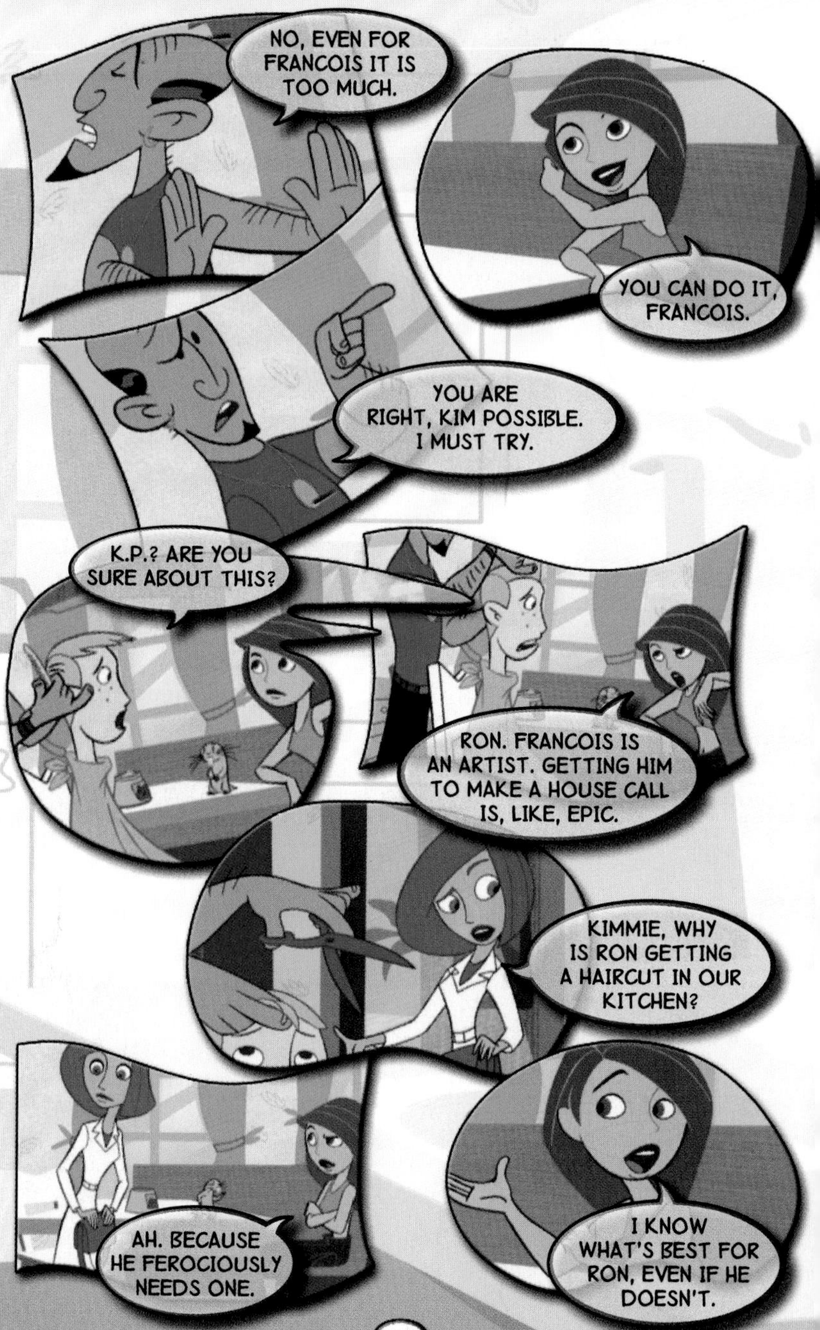
NO, EVEN FOR FRANCOIS IT IS TOO MUCH.
YOU CAN DO IT, FRANCOIS.
YOU ARE RIGHT, KIM POSSIBLE. I MUST TRY.
K.P.? ARE YOU SURE ABOUT THIS?
RON. FRANCOIS IS AN ARTIST. GETTING HIM TO MAKE A HOUSE CALL IS, LIKE, EPIC.
KIMMIE, WHY IS RON GETTING A HAIRCUT IN OUR KITCHEN?
AH. BECAUSE HE FEROCIOUSLY NEEDS ONE.
I KNOW WHAT'S BEST FOR RON, EVEN IF HE DOESN'T.

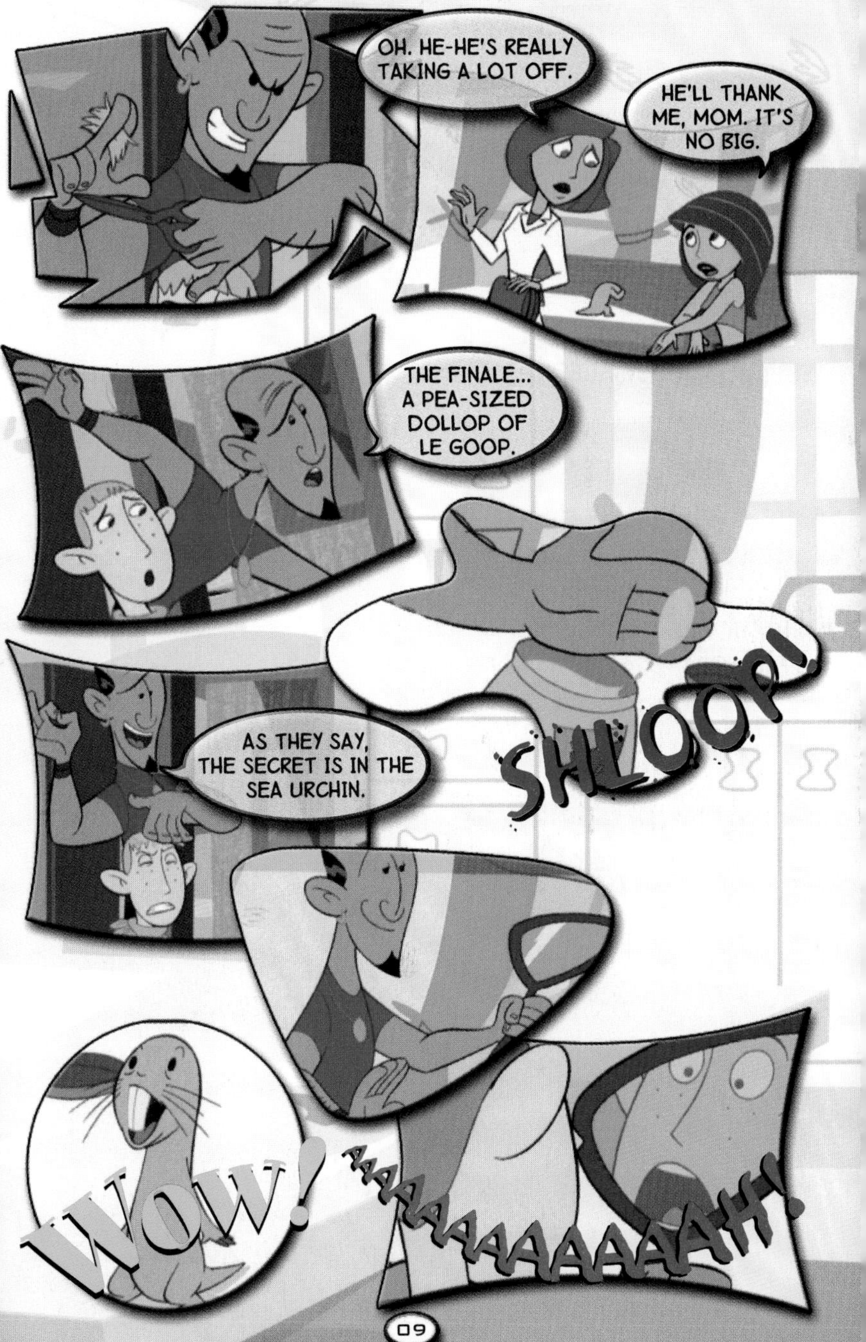
OH. HE-HE'S REALLY TAKING A LOT OFF.
HE'LL THANK ME, MOM. IT'S NO BIG.
THE FINALE... A PEA-SIZED DOLLOP OF LE GOOP.
SHLOOP!
AS THEY SAY, THE SECRET IS IN THE SEA URCHIN.
WOW!
AAAAAAAAAAAH!

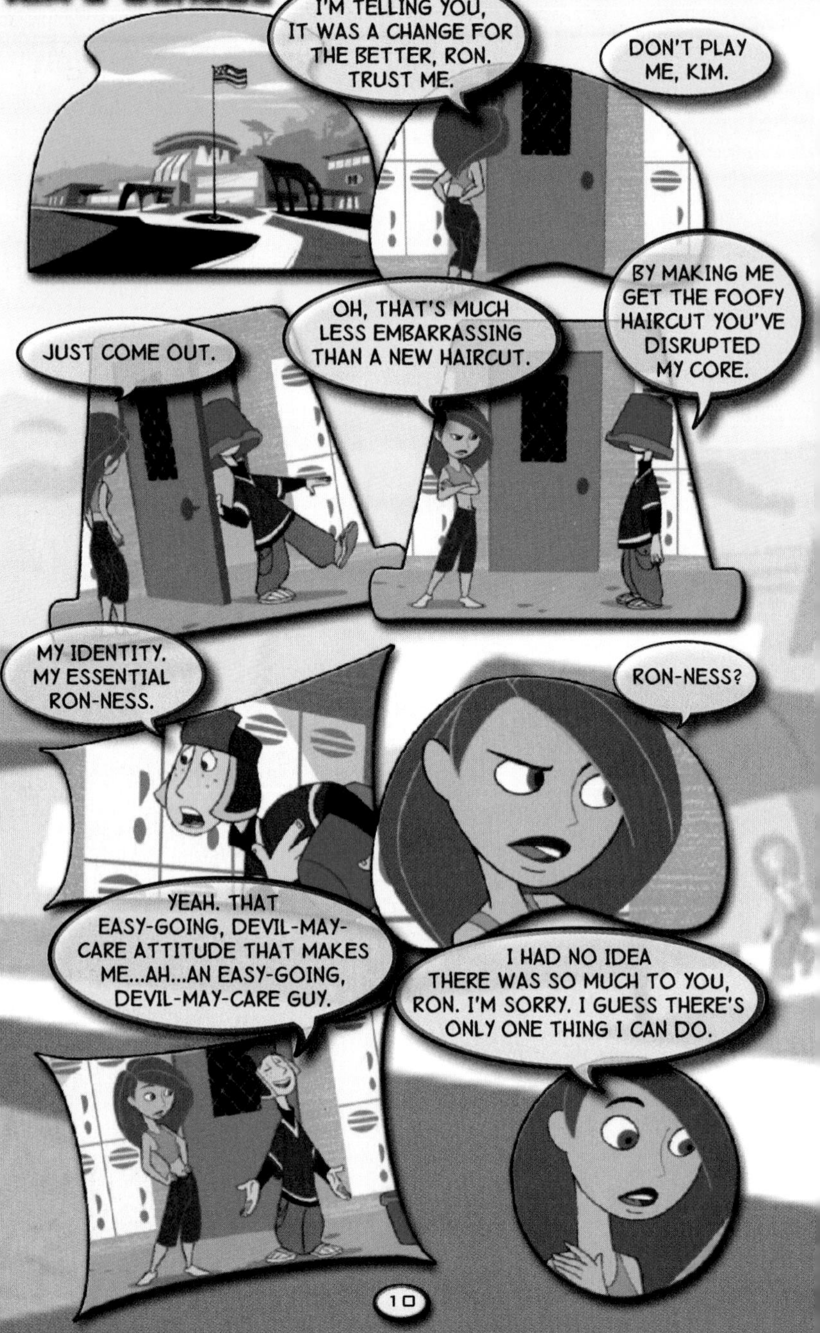
I'M TELLING YOU, IT WAS A CHANGE FOR THE BETTER, RON. TRUST ME.
DON'T PLAY ME, KIM.
JUST COME OUT.
OH, THAT'S MUCH LESS EMBARRASSING THAN A NEW HAIRCUT.
BY MAKING ME GET THE FOOFY HAIRCUT YOU'VE DISRUPTED MY CORE.
MY IDENTITY. MY ESSENTIAL RON-NESS.
RON-NESS?
YEAH. THAT EASY-GOING, DEVIL-MAY-CARE ATTITUDE THAT MAKES ME...AH...AN EASY-GOING, DEVIL-MAY-CARE GUY.
I HAD NO IDEA THERE WAS SO MUCH TO YOU, RON. I'M SORRY. I GUESS THERE'S ONLY ONE THING I CAN DO.

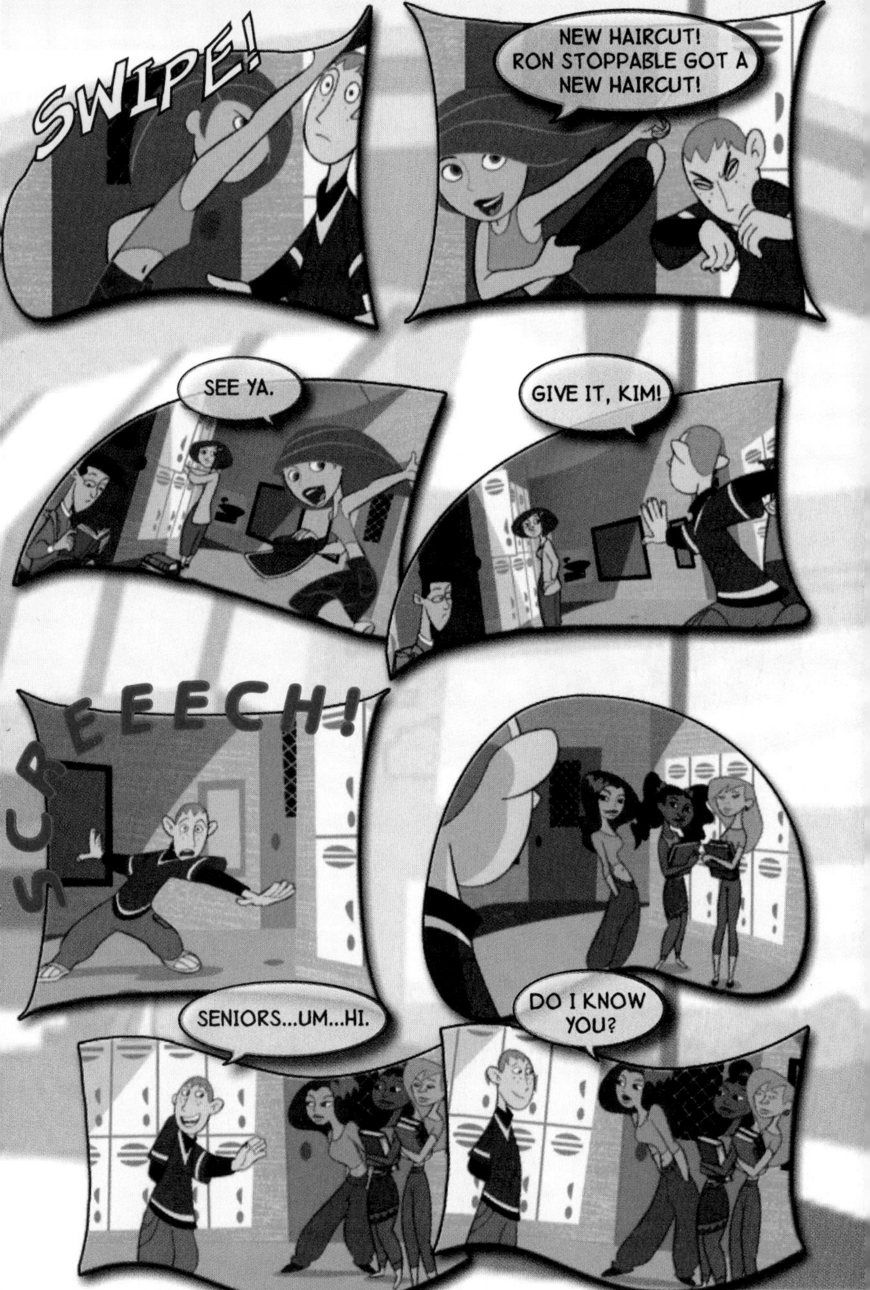
SWIPE!
NEW HAIRCUT! RON STOPPABLE GOT A NEW HAIRCUT!
SEE YA.
GIVE IT, KIM!
SCREEECH!
SENIORS...UM...HI.
DO I KNOW YOU?

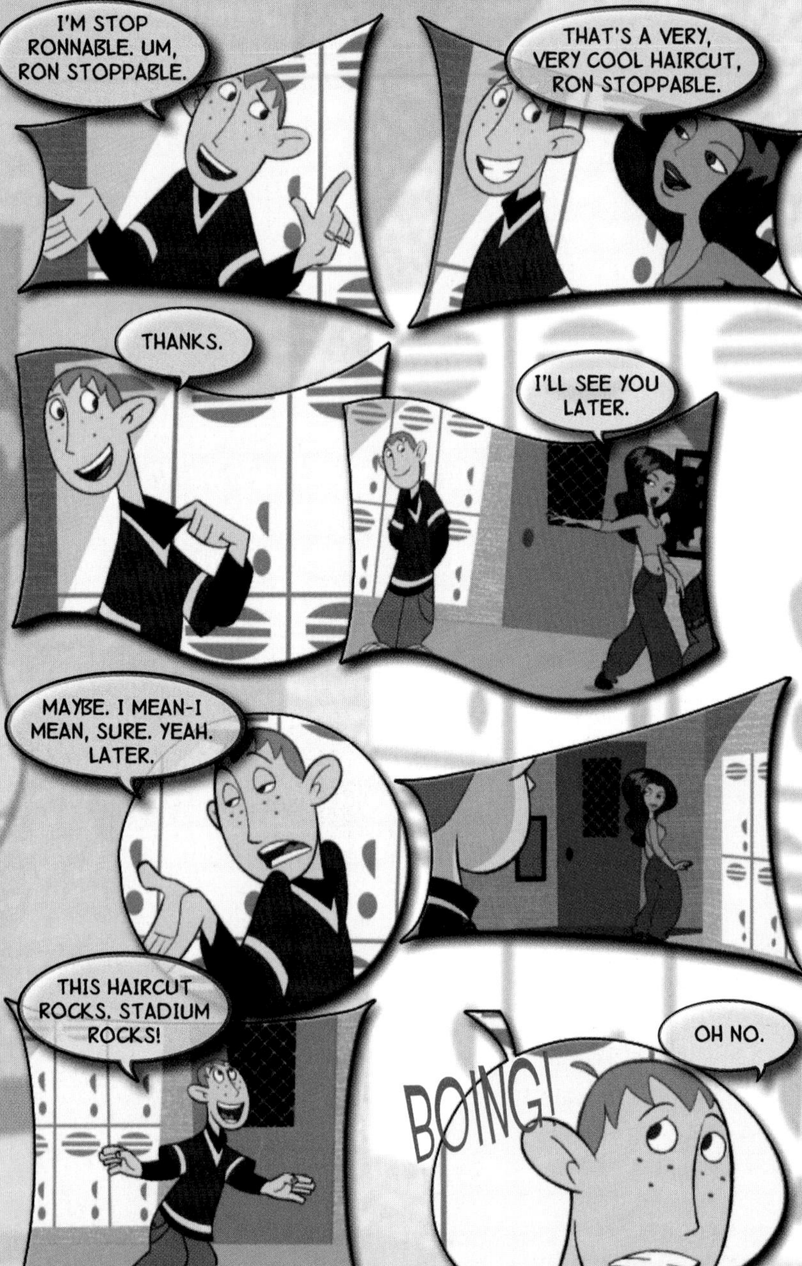
I'M STOP RONNABLE. UM, RON STOPPABLE.
THAT'S A VERY, VERY COOL HAIRCUT, RON STOPPABLE.
THANKS.
I'LL SEE YOU LATER.
MAYBE. I MEAN-I MEAN, SURE. YEAH. LATER.
THIS HAIRCUT ROCKS. STADIUM ROCKS!
BOING!
OH NO.

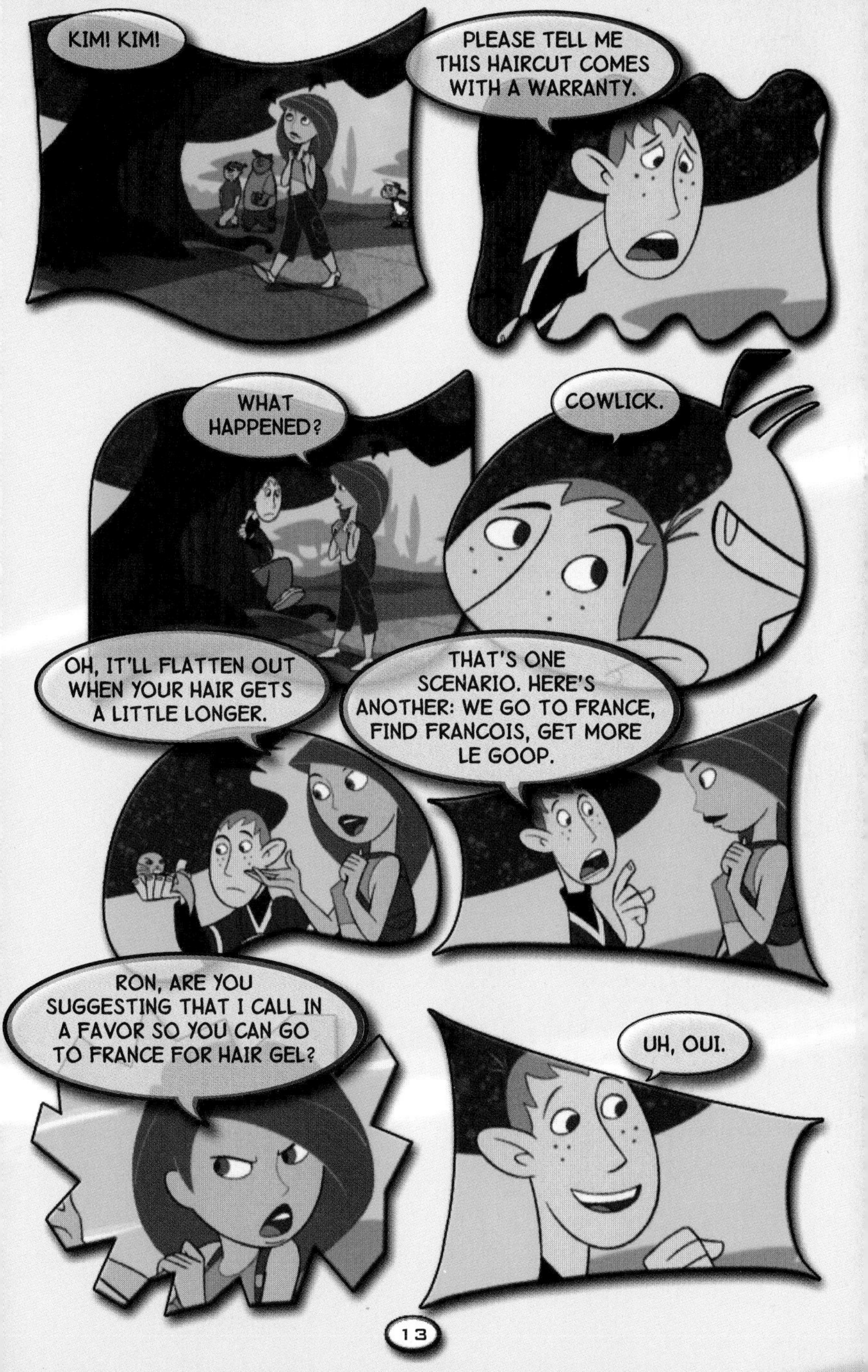
KIM! KIM!
PLEASE TELL ME THIS HAIRCUT COMES WITH A WARRANTY.
WHAT HAPPENED?
COWLICK.
OH, IT'LL FLATTEN OUT WHEN YOUR HAIR GETS A LITTLE LONGER.
THAT'S ONE SCENARIO. HERE'S ANOTHER: WE GO TO FRANCE, FIND FRANCOIS, GET MORE LE GOOP.
RON, ARE YOU SUGGESTING THAT I CALL IN A FAVOR SO YOU CAN GO TO FRANCE FOR HAIR GEL?
UH, OUI.

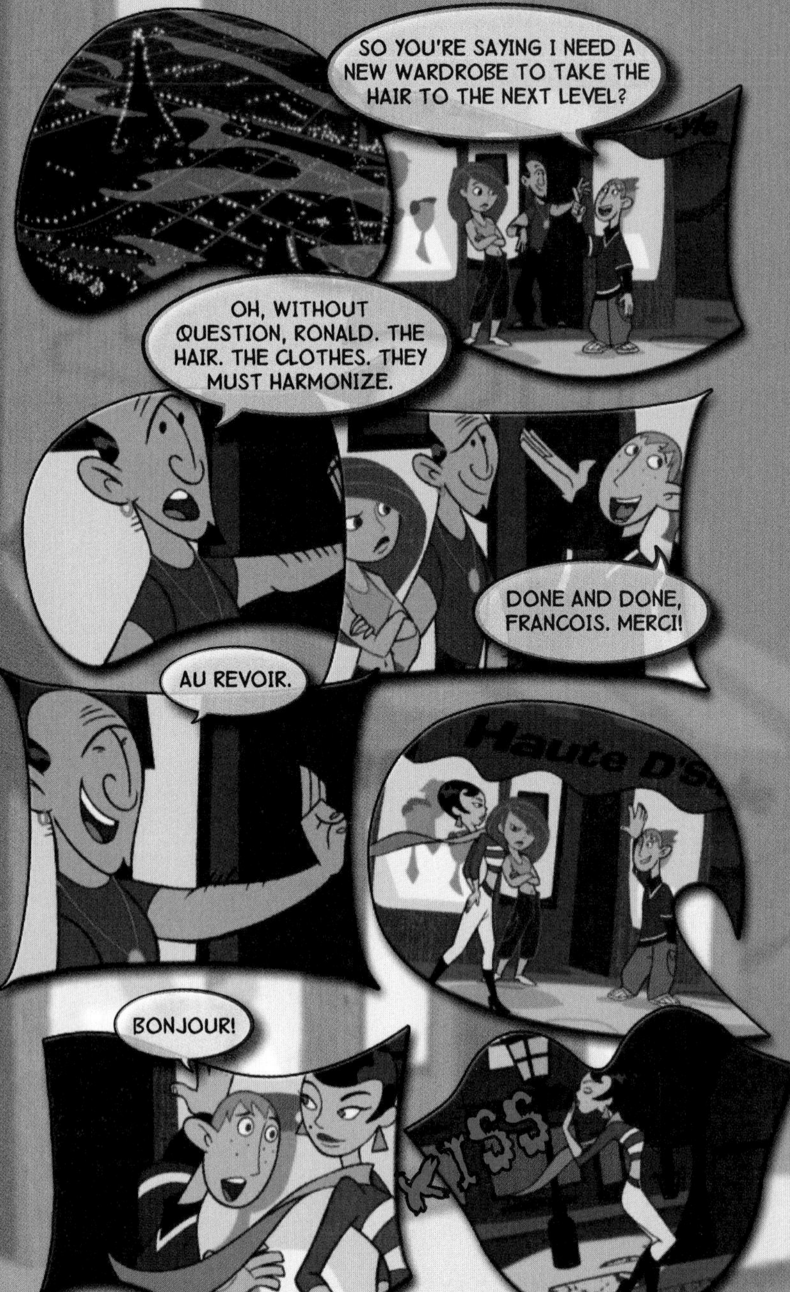
SO YOU'RE SAYING I NEED A NEW WARDROBE TO TAKE THE HAIR TO THE NEXT LEVEL?
OH, WITHOUT QUESTION, RONALD. THE HAIR. THE CLOTHES. THEY MUST HARMONIZE.
DONE AND DONE, FRANCOIS. MERCI!
AU REVOIR.
BONJOUR!
KISS

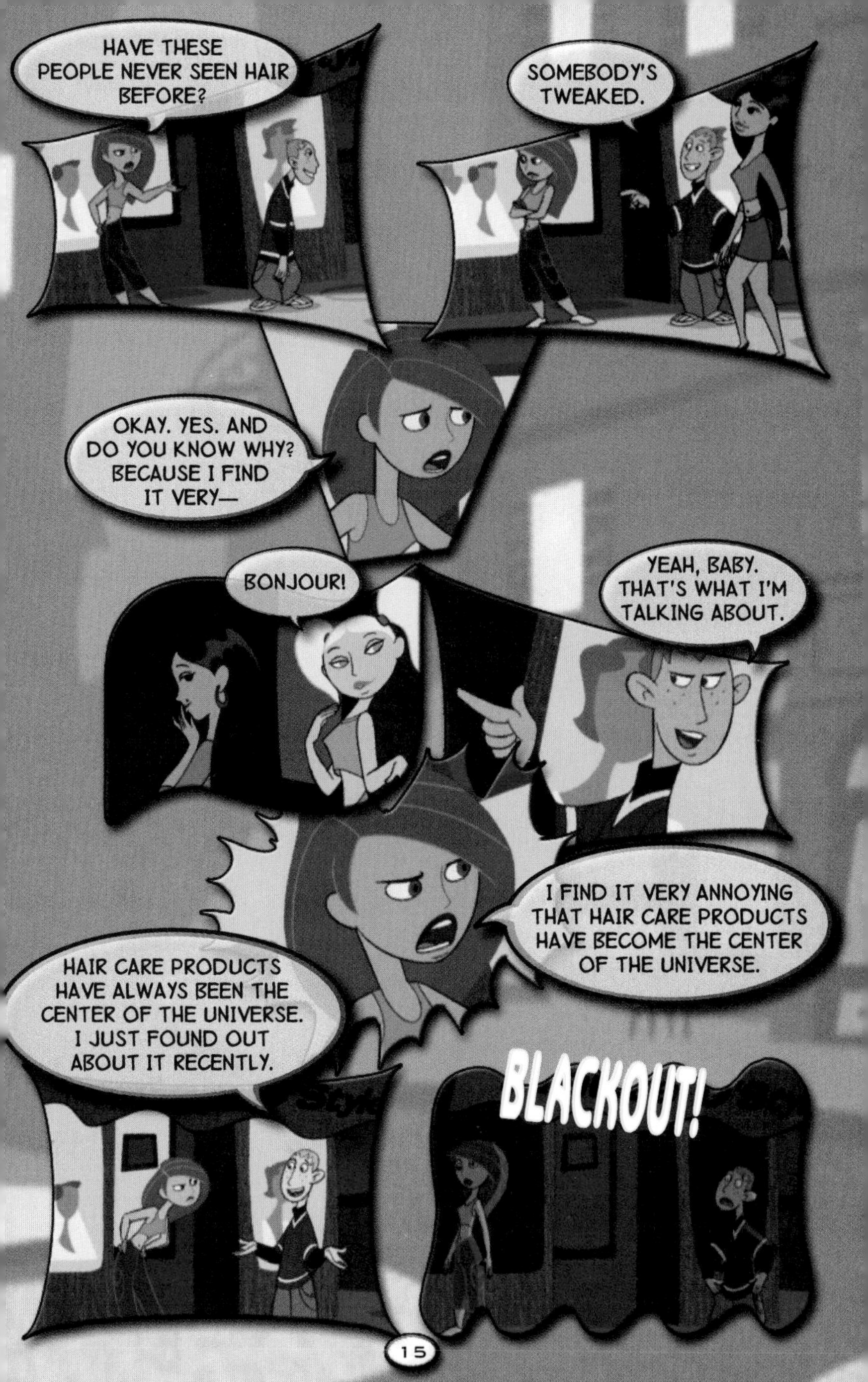
HAVE THESE PEOPLE NEVER SEEN HAIR BEFORE?
SOMEBODY'S TWEAKED.
OKAY. YES. AND DO YOU KNOW WHY? BECAUSE I FIND IT VERY—
BONJOUR!
YEAH, BABY. THAT'S WHAT I'M TALKING ABOUT.
I FIND IT VERY ANNOYING THAT HAIR CARE PRODUCTS HAVE BECOME THE CENTER OF THE UNIVERSE.
HAIR CARE PRODUCTS HAVE ALWAYS BEEN THE CENTER OF THE UNIVERSE. I JUST FOUND OUT ABOUT IT RECENTLY.
BLACKOUT!

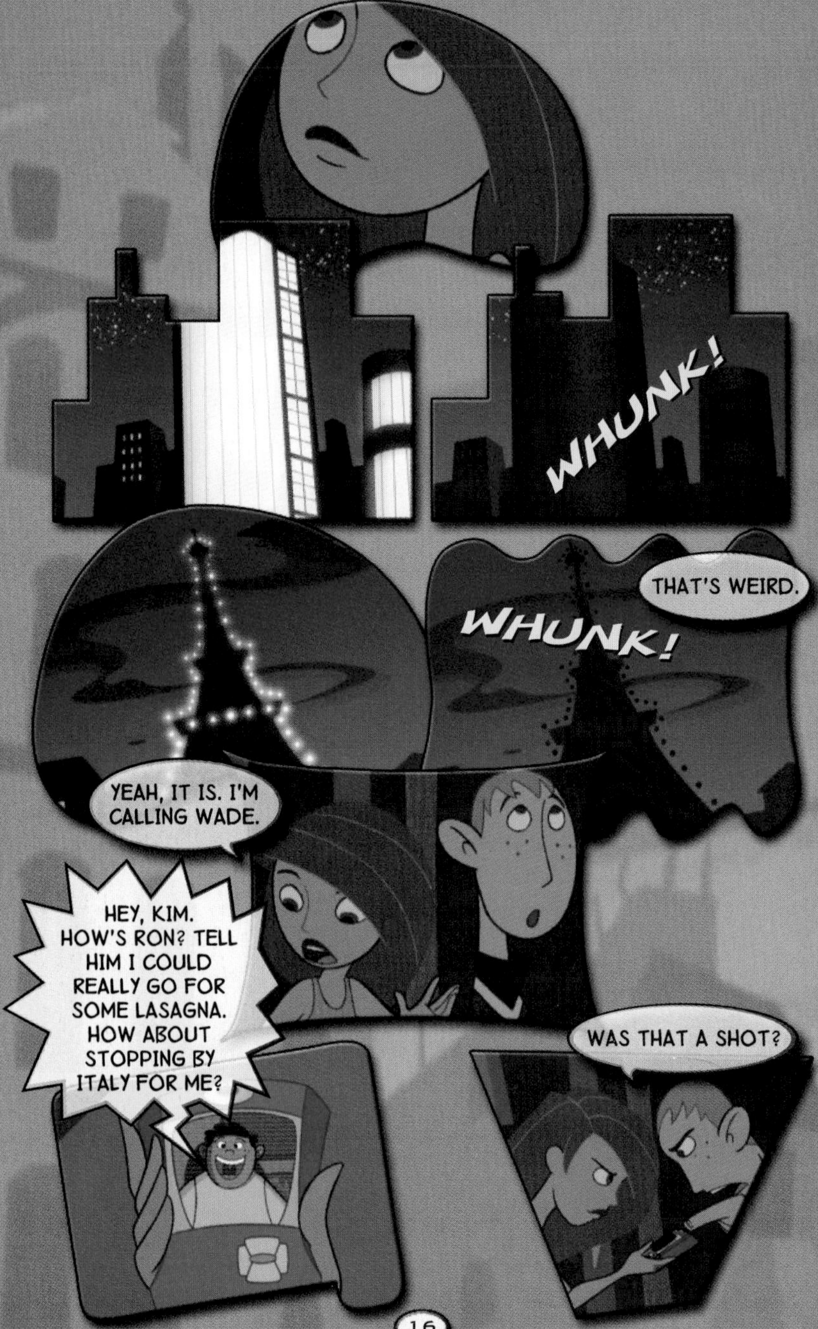
WHUNK!
THAT'S WEIRD.
WHUNK!
YEAH, IT IS. I'M CALLING WADE.
HEY, KIM. HOW'S RON? TELL HIM I COULD REALLY GO FOR SOME LASAGNA. HOW ABOUT STOPPING BY ITALY FOR ME?
WAS THAT A SHOT?

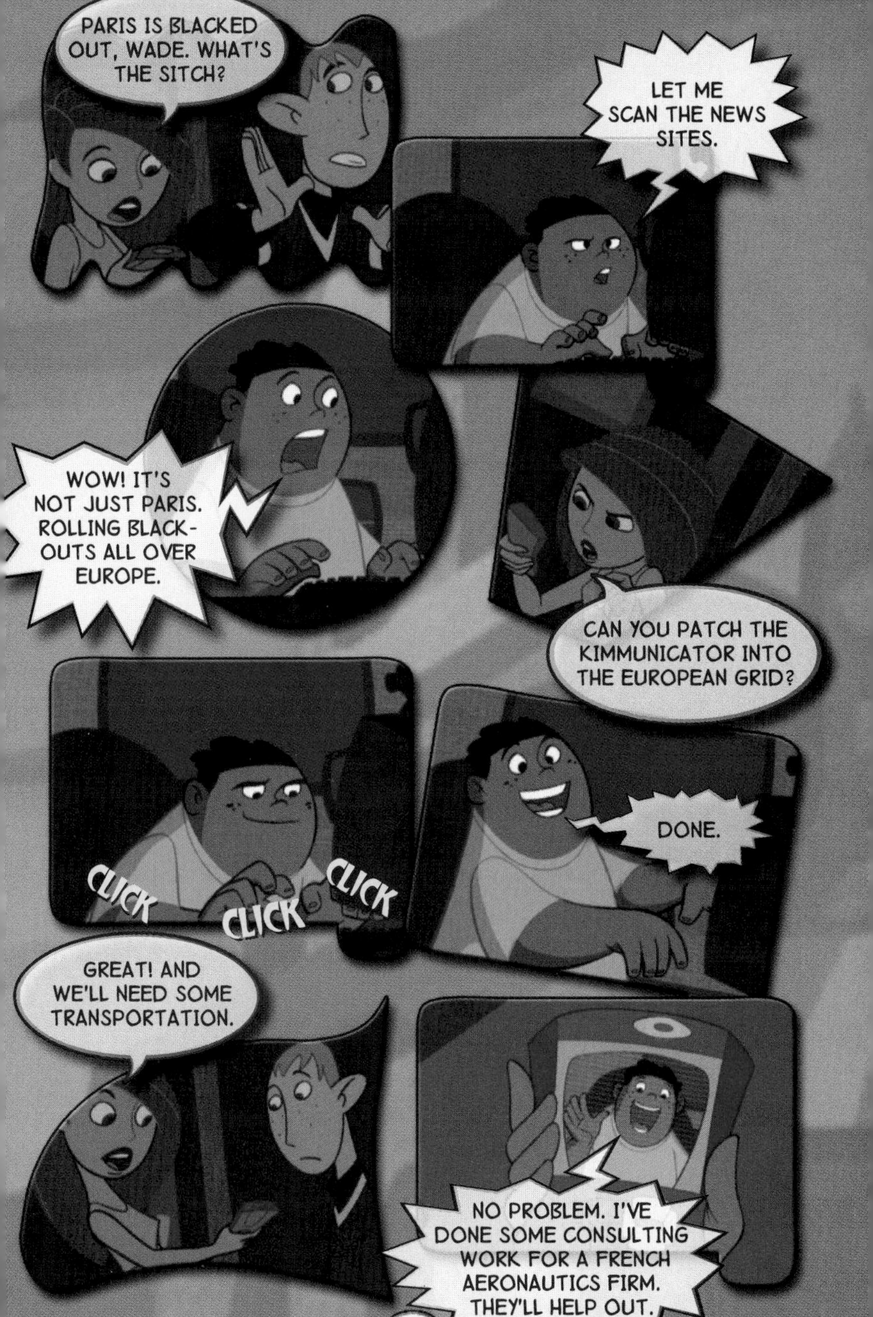
PARIS IS BLACKED OUT, WADE. WHAT'S THE SITCH?
LET ME SCAN THE NEWS SITES.
WOW! IT'S NOT JUST PARIS. ROLLING BLACK-OUTS ALL OVER EUROPE.
CAN YOU PATCH THE KIMMUNICATOR INTO THE EUROPEAN GRID?
CLICK
CLICK
CLICK
DONE.
GREAT! AND WE'LL NEED SOME TRANSPORTATION.
NO PROBLEM. I'VE DONE SOME CONSULTING WORK FOR A FRENCH AERONAUTICS FIRM. THEY'LL HELP OUT.

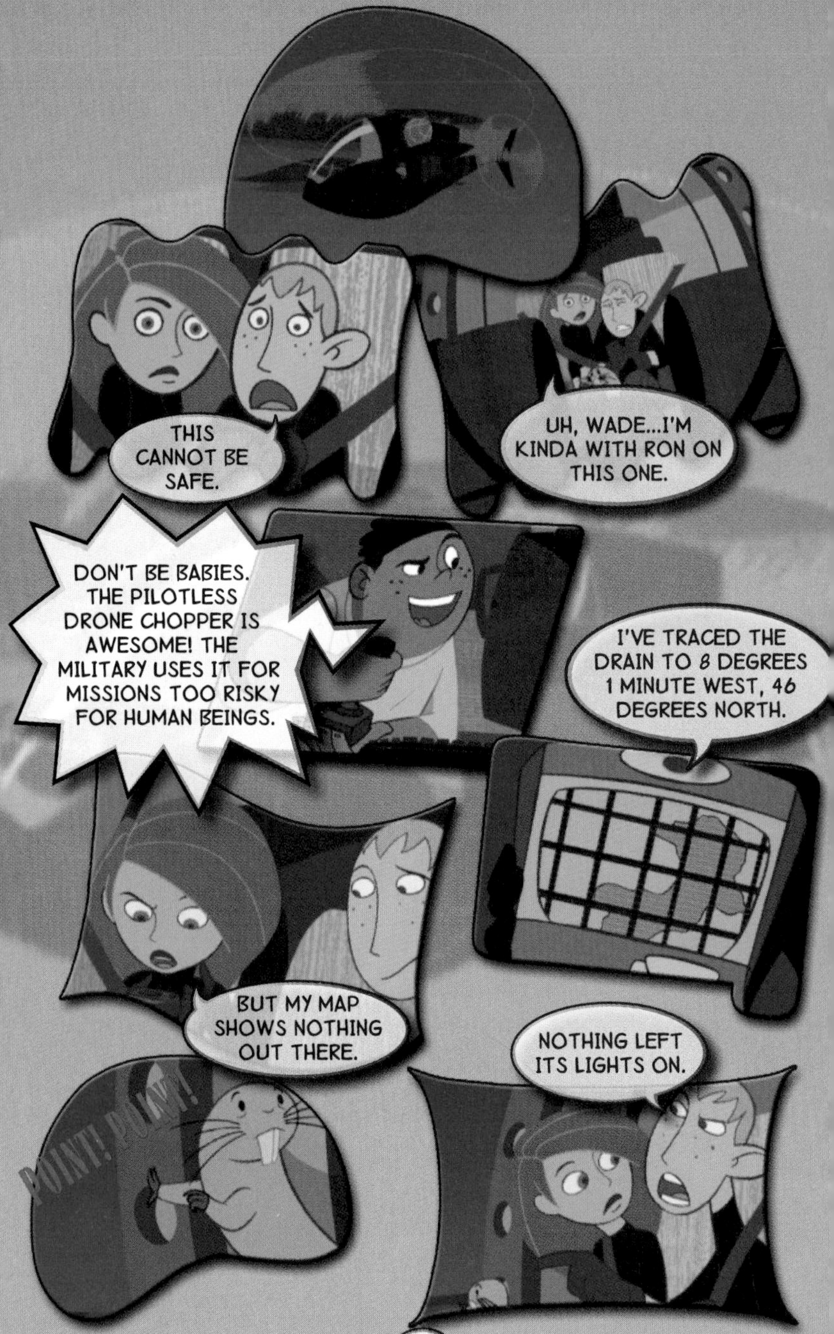
THIS CANNOT BE SAFE.
UH, WADE...I'M KINDA WITH RON ON THIS ONE.
DON'T BE BABIES. THE PILOTLESS DRONE CHOPPER IS AWESOME! THE MILITARY USES IT FOR MISSIONS TOO RISKY FOR HUMAN BEINGS.
I'VE TRACED THE DRAIN TO 8 DEGREES 1 MINUTE WEST, 46 DEGREES NORTH.
BUT MY MAP SHOWS NOTHING OUT THERE.
POINT! POINT!
NOTHING LEFT ITS LIGHTS ON.

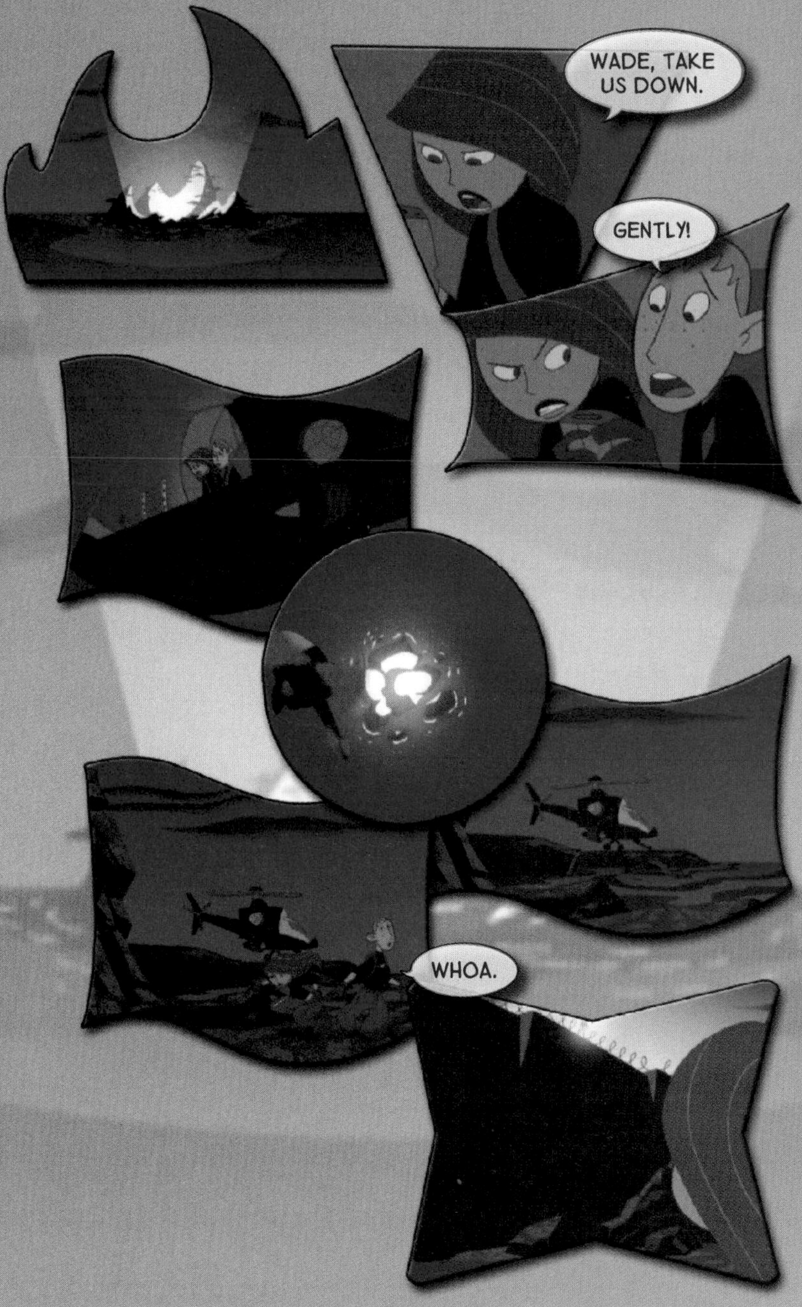
WADE, TAKE US DOWN.
GENTLY!
WHOA.

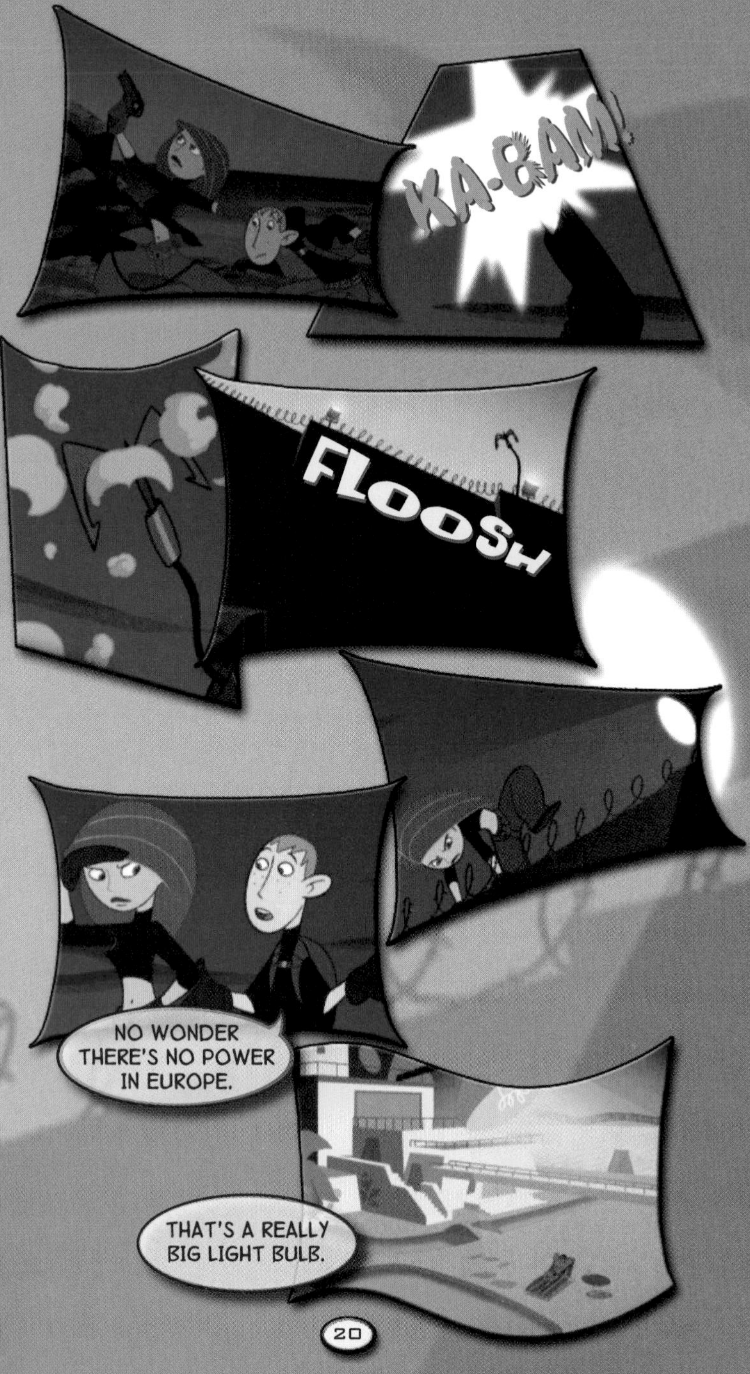
KA-BAM!
FLOOSH
NO WONDER THERE'S NO POWER IN EUROPE.
THAT'S A REALLY BIG LIGHT BULB.

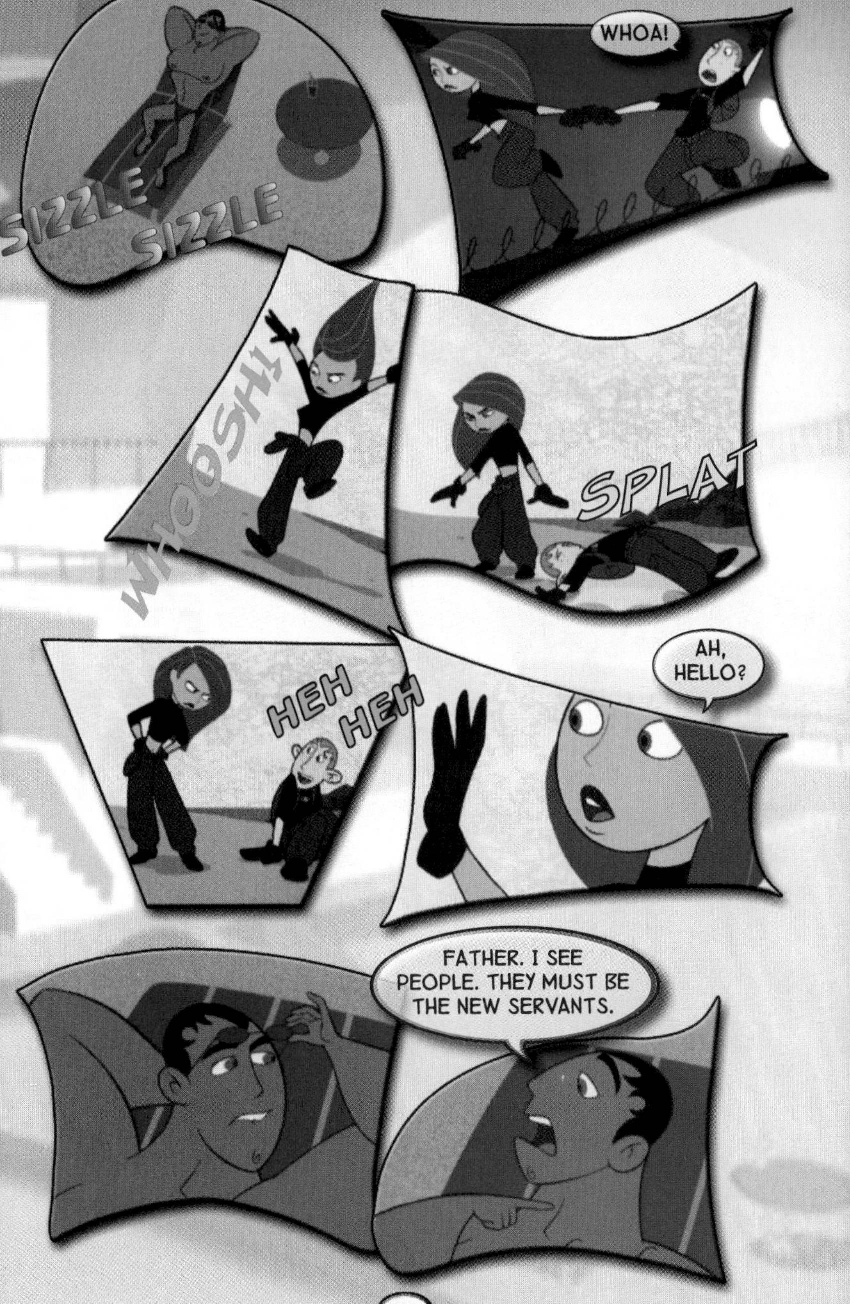
SIZZLE
SIZZLE
WHOA!
WHOOSH!
SPLAT
HEH
HEH
AH, HELLO?
FATHER. I SEE PEOPLE. THEY MUST BE THE NEW SERVANTS.

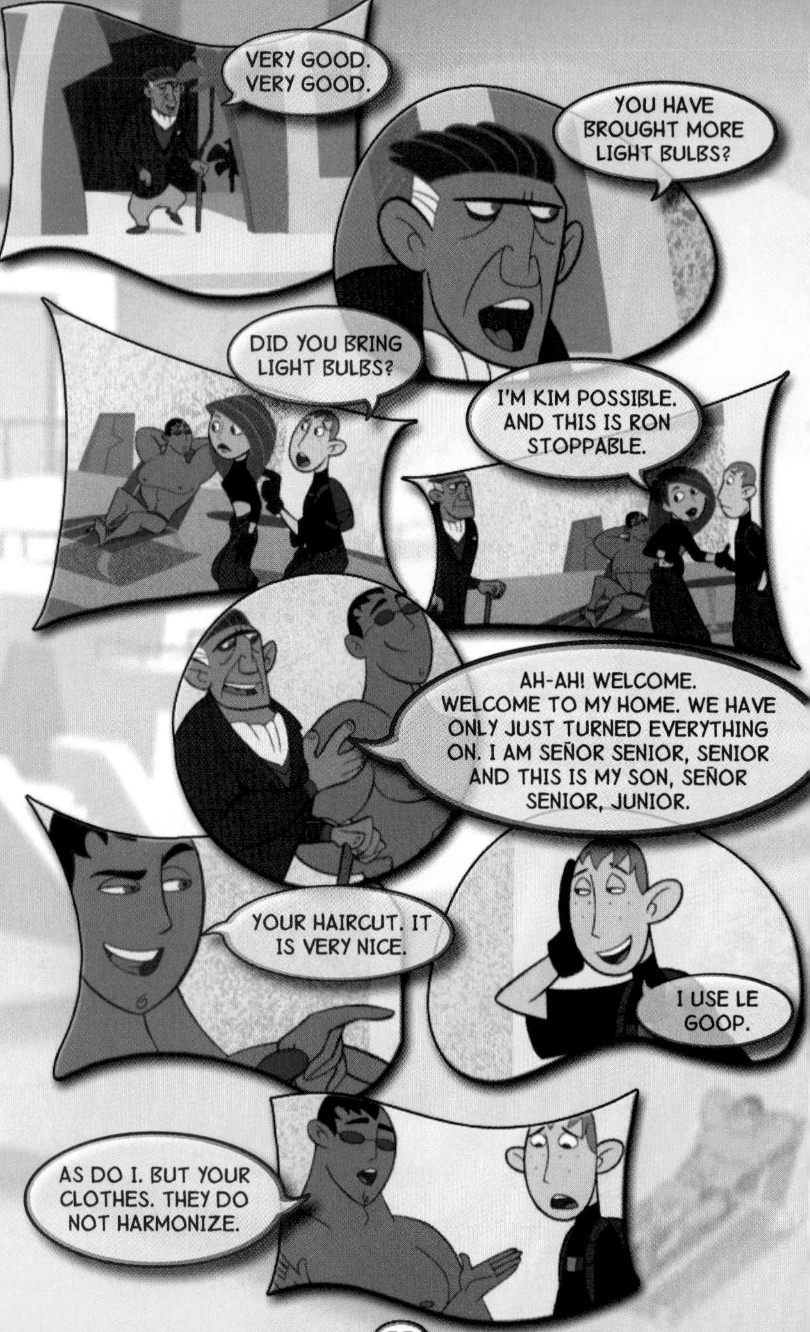
VERY GOOD. VERY GOOD.
YOU HAVE BROUGHT MORE LIGHT BULBS?
DID YOU BRING LIGHT BULBS?
I'M KIM POSSIBLE. AND THIS IS RON STOPPABLE.
AH-AH! WELCOME. WELCOME TO MY HOME. WE HAVE ONLY JUST TURNED EVERYTHING ON. I AM SEÑOR SENIOR, SENIOR AND THIS IS MY SON, SEÑOR SENIOR, JUNIOR.
YOUR HAIRCUT. IT IS VERY NICE.
I USE LE GOOP.
AS DO I. BUT YOUR CLOTHES. THEY DO NOT HARMONIZE.

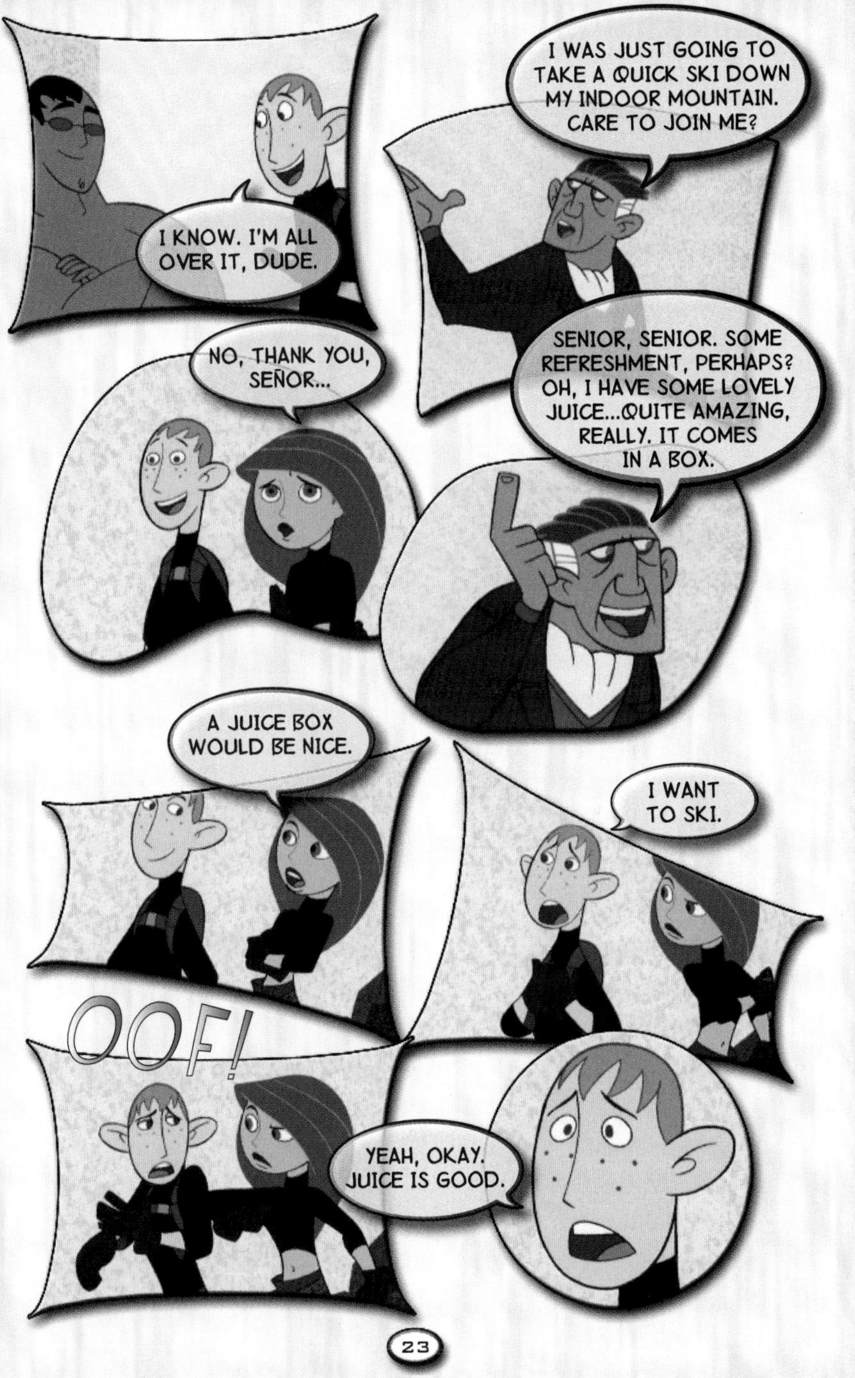
I KNOW. I'M ALL OVER IT, DUDE.
I WAS JUST GOING TO TAKE A QUICK SKI DOWN MY INDOOR MOUNTAIN. CARE TO JOIN ME?
NO, THANK YOU, SEÑOR...
SENIOR, SENIOR. SOME REFRESHMENT, PERHAPS? OH, I HAVE SOME LOVELY JUICE...QUITE AMAZING, REALLY. IT COMES IN A BOX.
A JUICE BOX WOULD BE NICE.
I WANT TO SKI.
OOF!
YEAH, OKAY. JUICE IS GOOD.

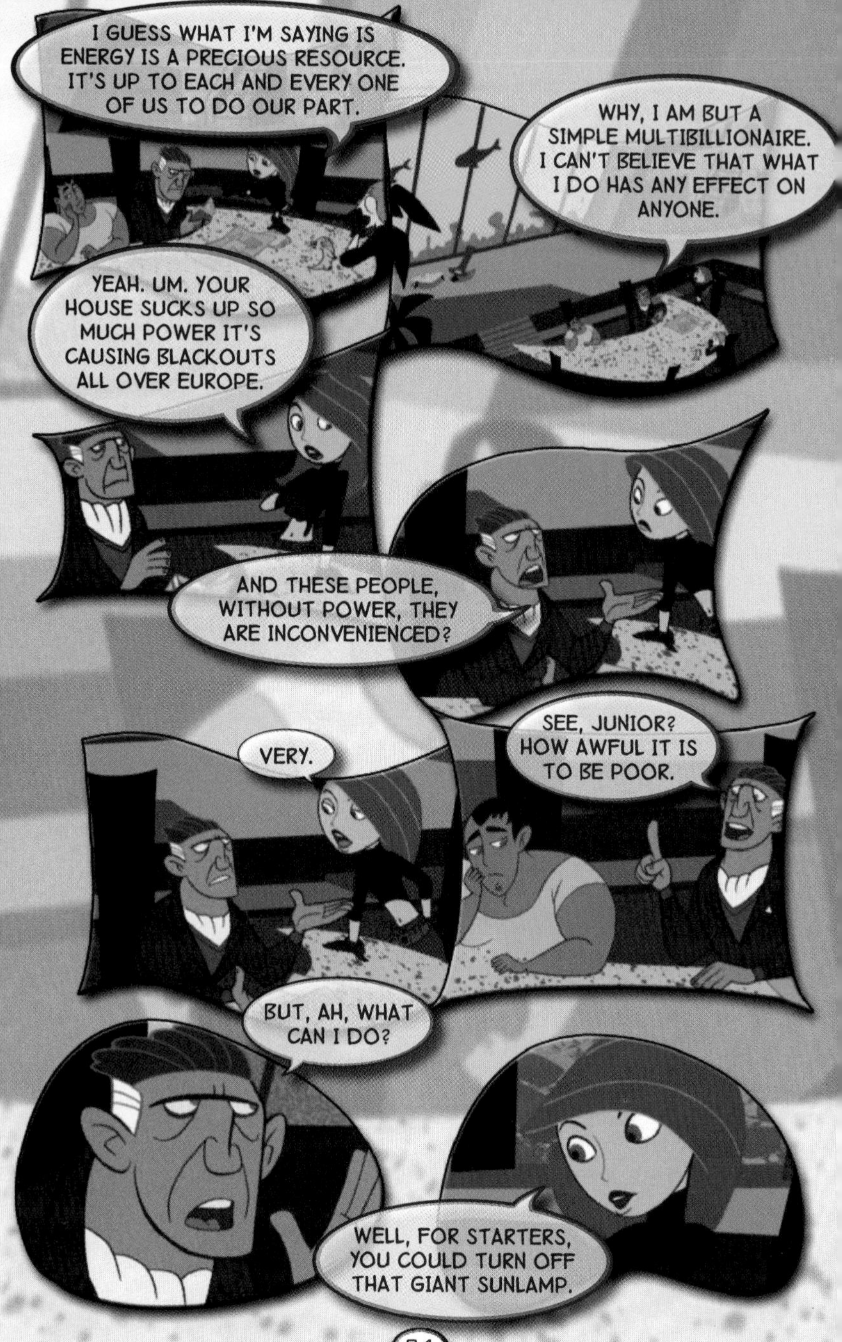
I GUESS WHAT I'M SAYING IS ENERGY IS A PRECIOUS RESOURCE. IT'S UP TO EACH AND EVERY ONE OF US TO DO OUR PART.
WHY, I AM BUT A SIMPLE MULTIBILLIONAIRE. I CAN'T BELIEVE THAT WHAT I DO HAS ANY EFFECT ON ANYONE.
YEAH. UM. YOUR HOUSE SUCKS UP SO MUCH POWER IT'S CAUSING BLACKOUTS ALL OVER EUROPE.
AND THESE PEOPLE, WITHOUT POWER, THEY ARE INCONVENIENCED?
VERY.
SEE, JUNIOR? HOW AWFUL IT IS TO BE POOR.
BUT, AH, WHAT CAN I DO?
WELL, FOR STARTERS, YOU COULD TURN OFF THAT GIANT SUNLAMP.

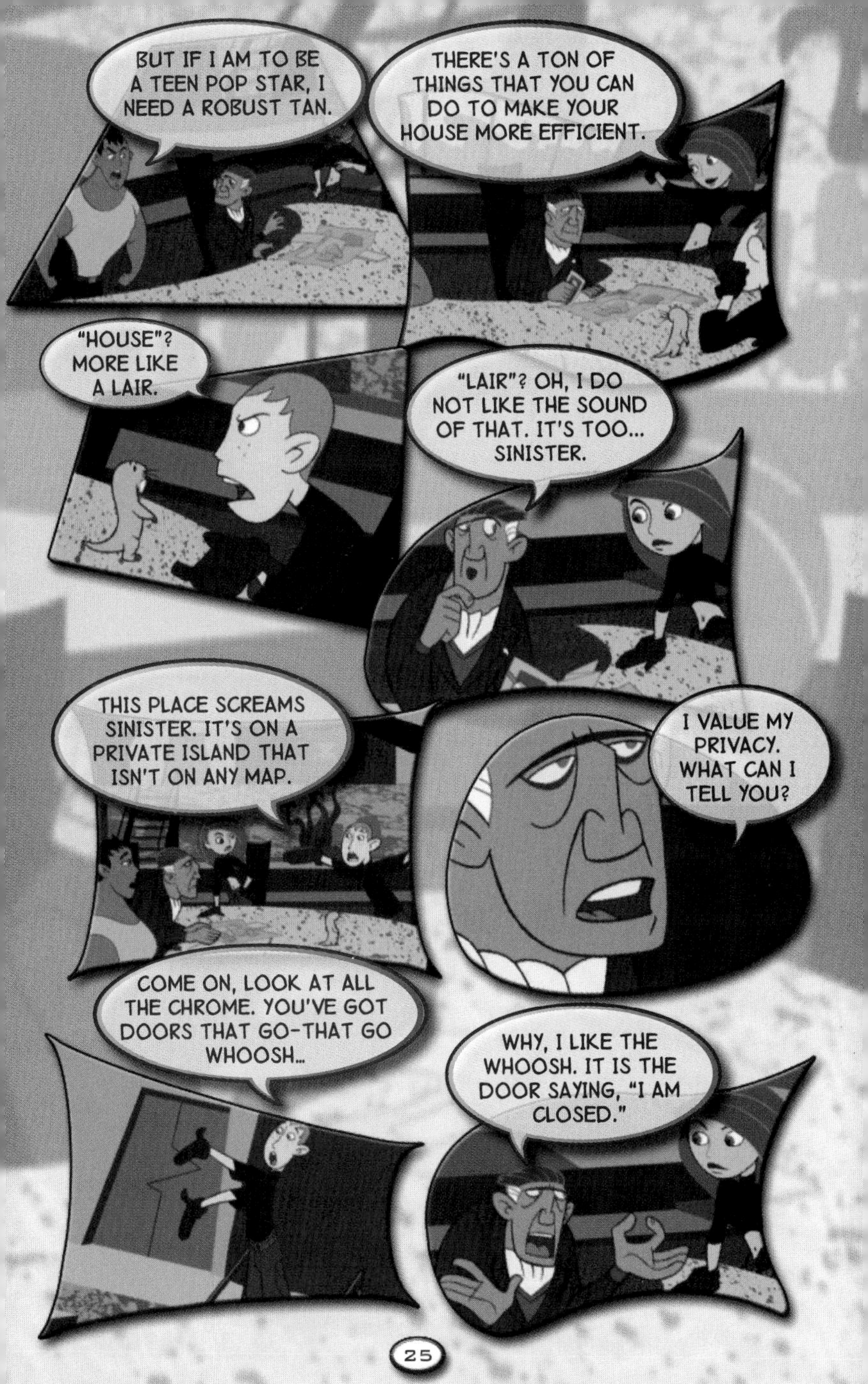
BUT IF I AM TO BE A TEEN POP STAR, I NEED A ROBUST TAN.
THERE'S A TON OF THINGS THAT YOU CAN DO TO MAKE YOUR HOUSE MORE EFFICIENT.
"HOUSE"? MORE LIKE A LAIR.
"LAIR"? OH, I DO NOT LIKE THE SOUND OF THAT. IT'S TOO... SINISTER.
THIS PLACE SCREAMS SINISTER. IT'S ON A PRIVATE ISLAND THAT ISN'T ON ANY MAP.
I VALUE MY PRIVACY. WHAT CAN I TELL YOU?
COME ON, LOOK AT ALL THE CHROME. YOU'VE GOT DOORS THAT GO-THAT GO WHOOSH...
WHY, I LIKE THE WHOOSH. IT IS THE DOOR SAYING, "I AM CLOSED."

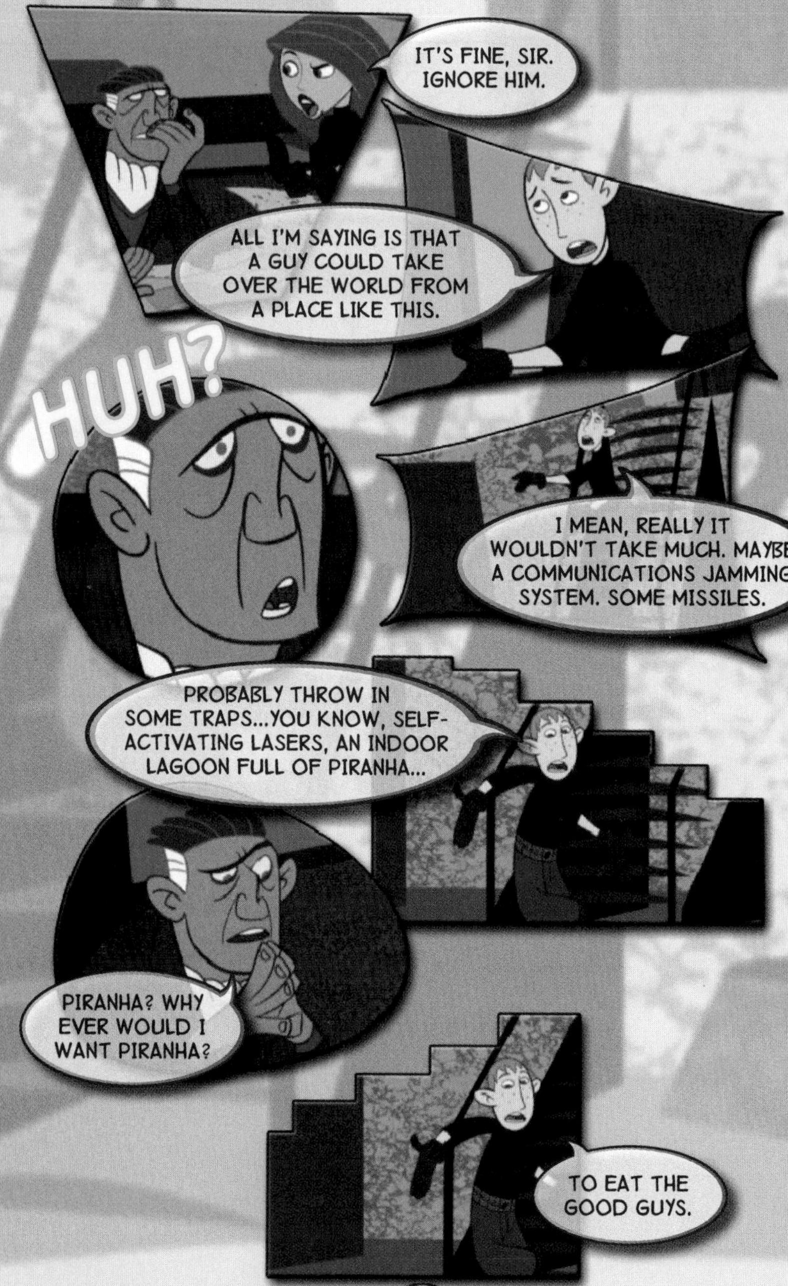
IT'S FINE, SIR. IGNORE HIM.
ALL I'M SAYING IS THAT A GUY COULD TAKE OVER THE WORLD FROM A PLACE LIKE THIS.
HUH?
I MEAN, REALLY IT WOULDN'T TAKE MUCH. MAYBE A COMMUNICATIONS JAMMING SYSTEM. SOME MISSILES.
PROBABLY THROW IN SOME TRAPS...YOU KNOW, SELF-ACTIVATING LASERS, AN INDOOR LAGOON FULL OF PIRANHA...
PIRANHA? WHY EVER WOULD I WANT PIRANHA?
TO EAT THE GOOD GUYS.

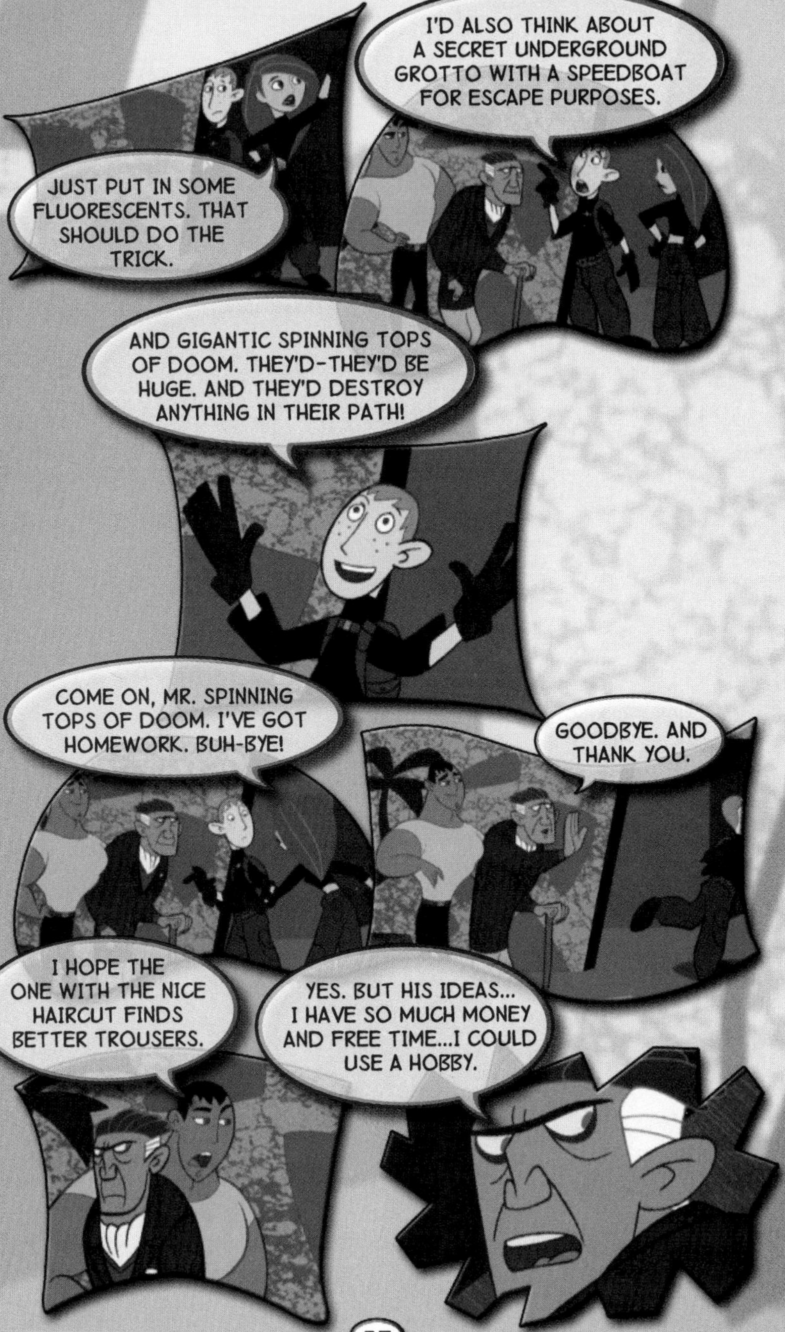
JUST PUT IN SOME FLUORESCENTS. THAT SHOULD DO THE TRICK.
I'D ALSO THINK ABOUT A SECRET UNDERGROUND GROTTO WITH A SPEEDBOAT FOR ESCAPE PURPOSES.
AND GIGANTIC SPINNING TOPS OF DOOM. THEY'D-THEY'D BE HUGE. AND THEY'D DESTROY ANYTHING IN THEIR PATH!
COME ON, MR. SPINNING TOPS OF DOOM. I'VE GOT HOMEWORK. BUH-BYE!
GOODBYE. AND THANK YOU.
I HOPE THE ONE WITH THE NICE HAIRCUT FINDS BETTER TROUSERS.
YES. BUT HIS IDEAS... I HAVE SO MUCH MONEY AND FREE TIME...I COULD USE A HOBBY.

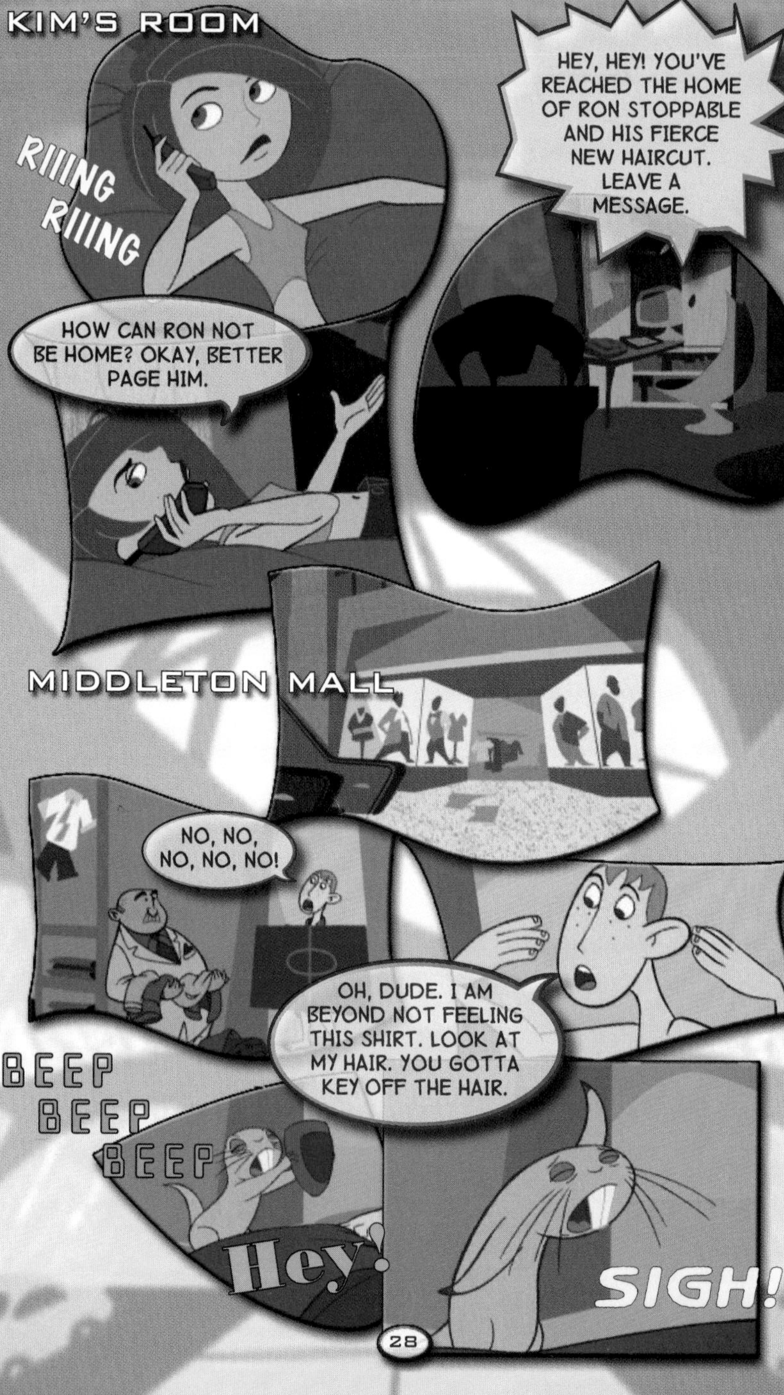
KIM'S ROOM
RIIING RIIING
HEY, HEY! YOU'VE REACHED THE HOME OF RON STOPPABLE AND HIS FIERCE NEW HAIRCUT. LEAVE A MESSAGE.
HOW CAN RON NOT BE HOME? OKAY, BETTER PAGE HIM.
MIDDLETON MALL
NO, NO, NO, NO, NO!
OH, DUDE. I AM BEYOND NOT FEELING THIS SHIRT. LOOK AT MY HAIR. YOU GOTTA KEY OFF THE HAIR.
BEEP BEEP BEEP
Hey!
SIGH!

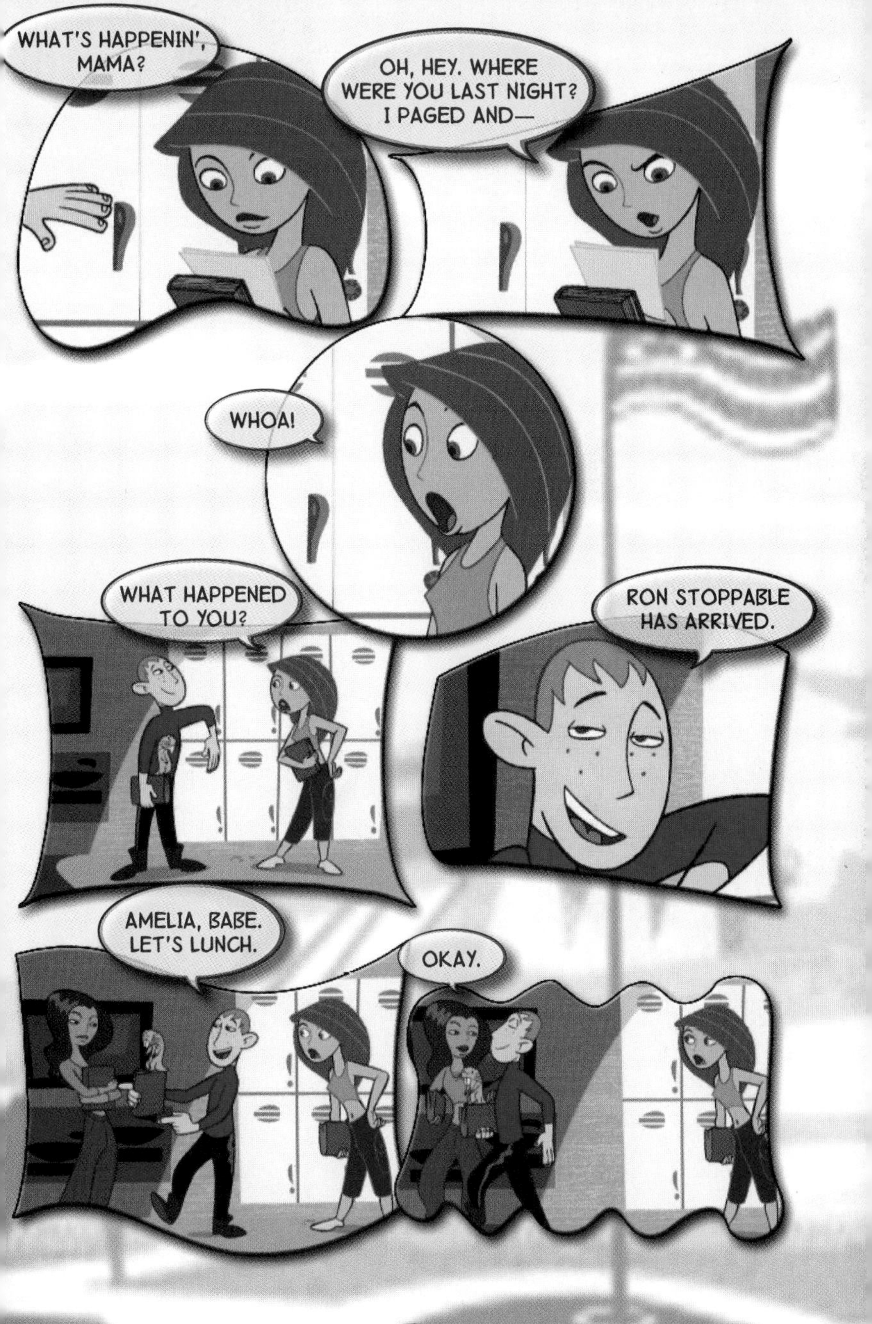
WHAT'S HAPPENIN', MAMA?
OH, HEY. WHERE WERE YOU LAST NIGHT? I PAGED AND—
WHOA!
WHAT HAPPENED TO YOU?
RON STOPPABLE HAS ARRIVED.
AMELIA, BABE. LET'S LUNCH.
OKAY.

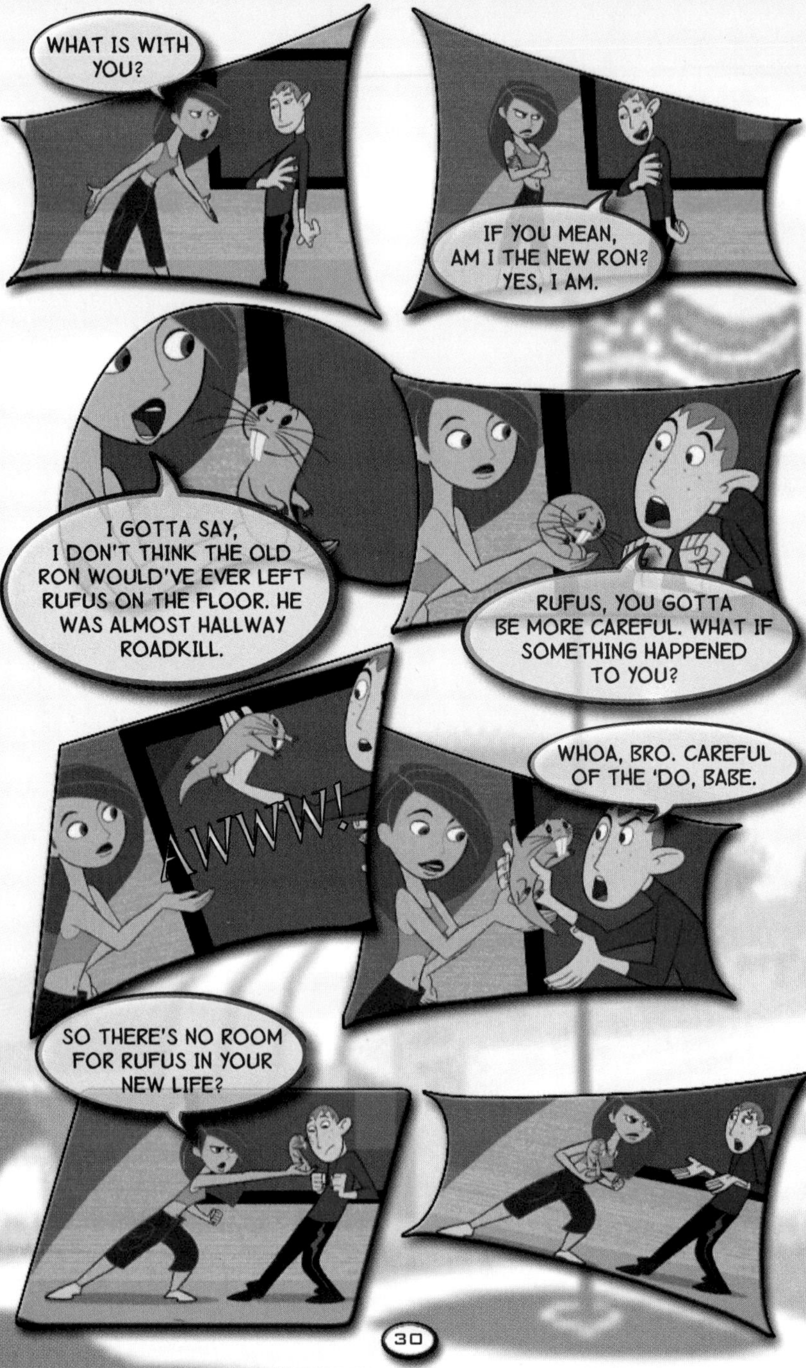
WHAT IS WITH YOU?
IF YOU MEAN, AM I THE NEW RON? YES, I AM.
I GOTTA SAY, I DON'T THINK THE OLD RON WOULD'VE EVER LEFT RUFUS ON THE FLOOR. HE WAS ALMOST HALLWAY ROADKILL.
RUFUS, YOU GOTTA BE MORE CAREFUL. WHAT IF SOMETHING HAPPENED TO YOU?
AWWW!
WHOA, BRO. CAREFUL OF THE 'DO, BABE.
SO THERE'S NO ROOM FOR RUFUS IN YOUR NEW LIFE?

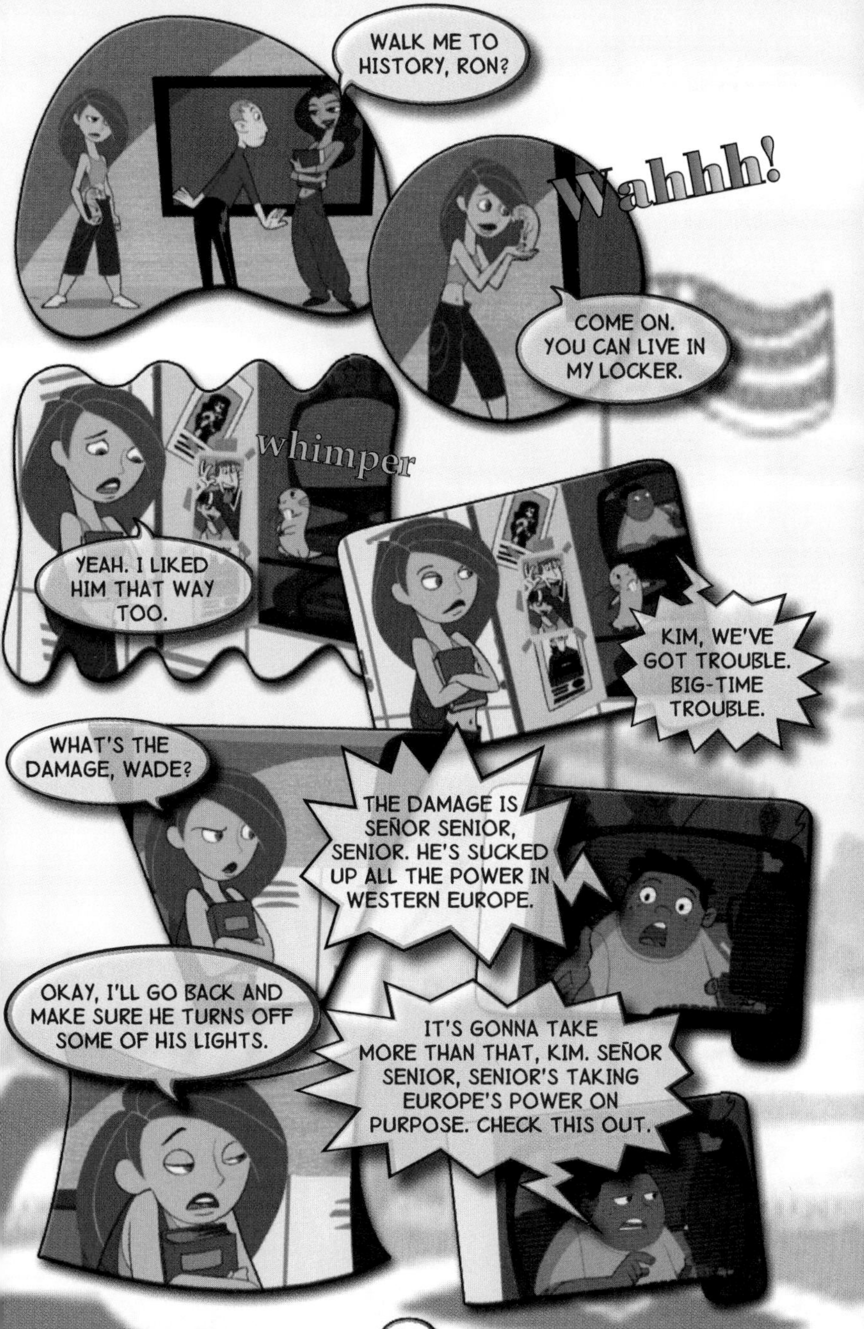
WALK ME TO HISTORY, RON?
Wahhh!
COME ON. YOU CAN LIVE IN MY LOCKER.
whimper
YEAH. I LIKED HIM THAT WAY TOO.
KIM, WE'VE GOT TROUBLE. BIG-TIME TROUBLE.
WHAT'S THE DAMAGE, WADE?
THE DAMAGE IS SEÑOR SENIOR, SENIOR. HE'S SUCKED UP ALL THE POWER IN WESTERN EUROPE.
OKAY, I'LL GO BACK AND MAKE SURE HE TURNS OFF SOME OF HIS LIGHTS.
IT'S GONNA TAKE MORE THAN THAT, KIM. SEÑOR SENIOR, SENIOR'S TAKING EUROPE'S POWER ON PURPOSE. CHECK THIS OUT.

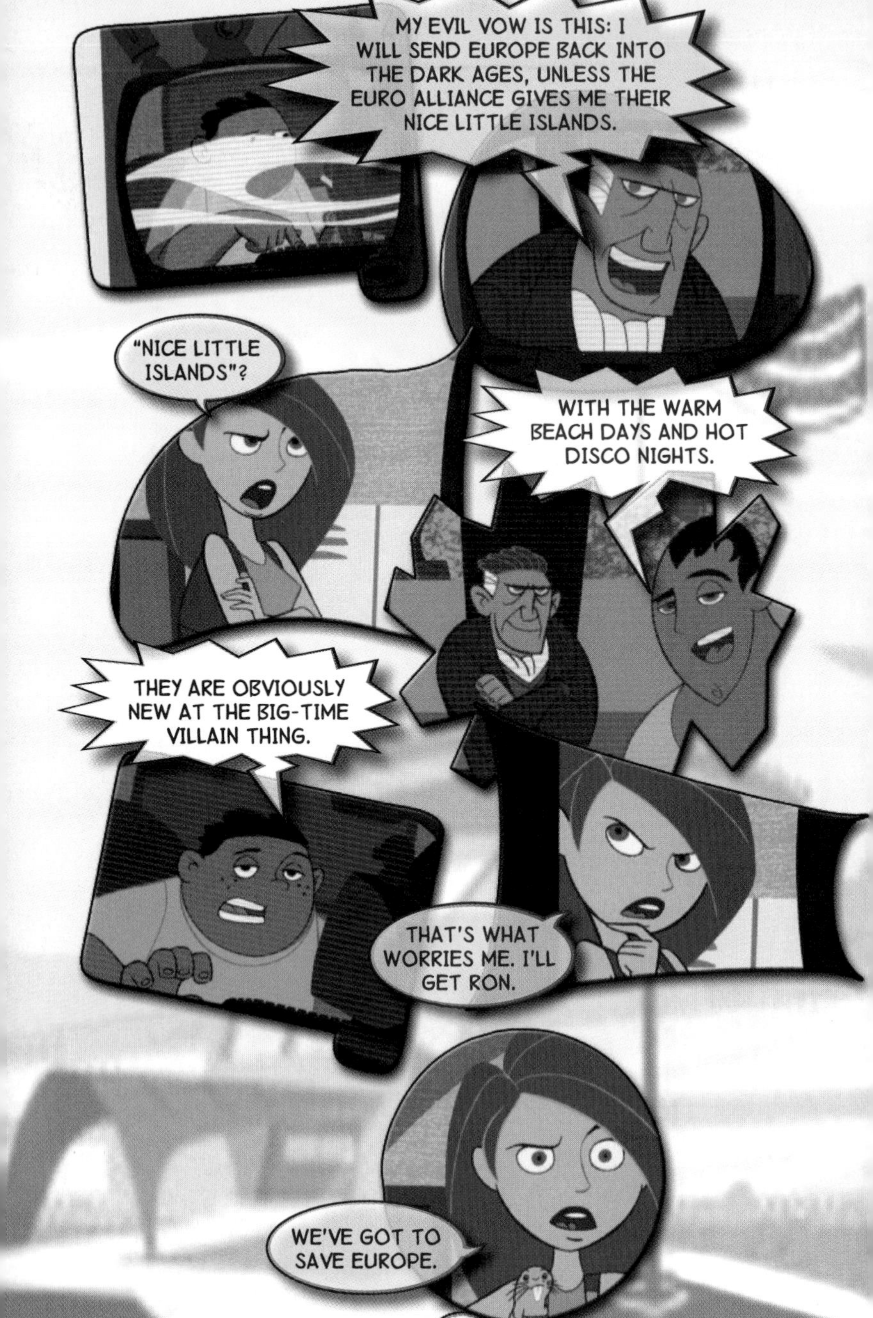
MY EVIL VOW IS THIS: I WILL SEND EUROPE BACK INTO THE DARK AGES, UNLESS THE EURO ALLIANCE GIVES ME THEIR NICE LITTLE ISLANDS.
"NICE LITTLE ISLANDS"?
WITH THE WARM BEACH DAYS AND HOT DISCO NIGHTS.
THEY ARE OBVIOUSLY NEW AT THE BIG-TIME VILLAIN THING.
THAT'S WHAT WORRIES ME. I'LL GET RON.
WE'VE GOT TO SAVE EUROPE.

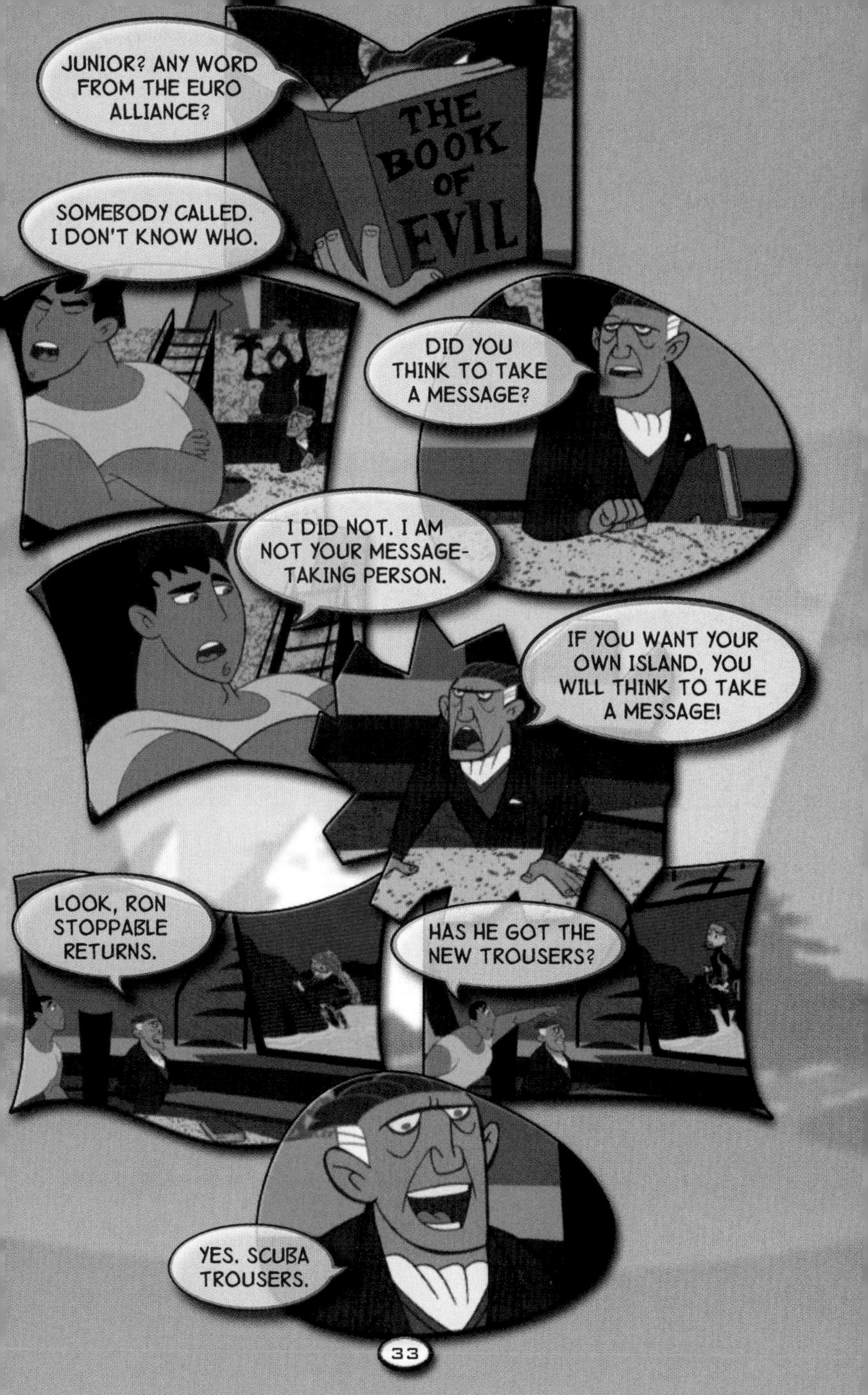
JUNIOR? ANY WORD FROM THE EURO ALLIANCE?
THE BOOK OF EVIL
SOMEBODY CALLED. I DON'T KNOW WHO.
DID YOU THINK TO TAKE A MESSAGE?
I DID NOT. I AM NOT YOUR MESSAGE-TAKING PERSON.
IF YOU WANT YOUR OWN ISLAND, YOU WILL THINK TO TAKE A MESSAGE!
LOOK, RON STOPPABLE RETURNS.
HAS HE GOT THE NEW TROUSERS?
YES. SCUBA TROUSERS.

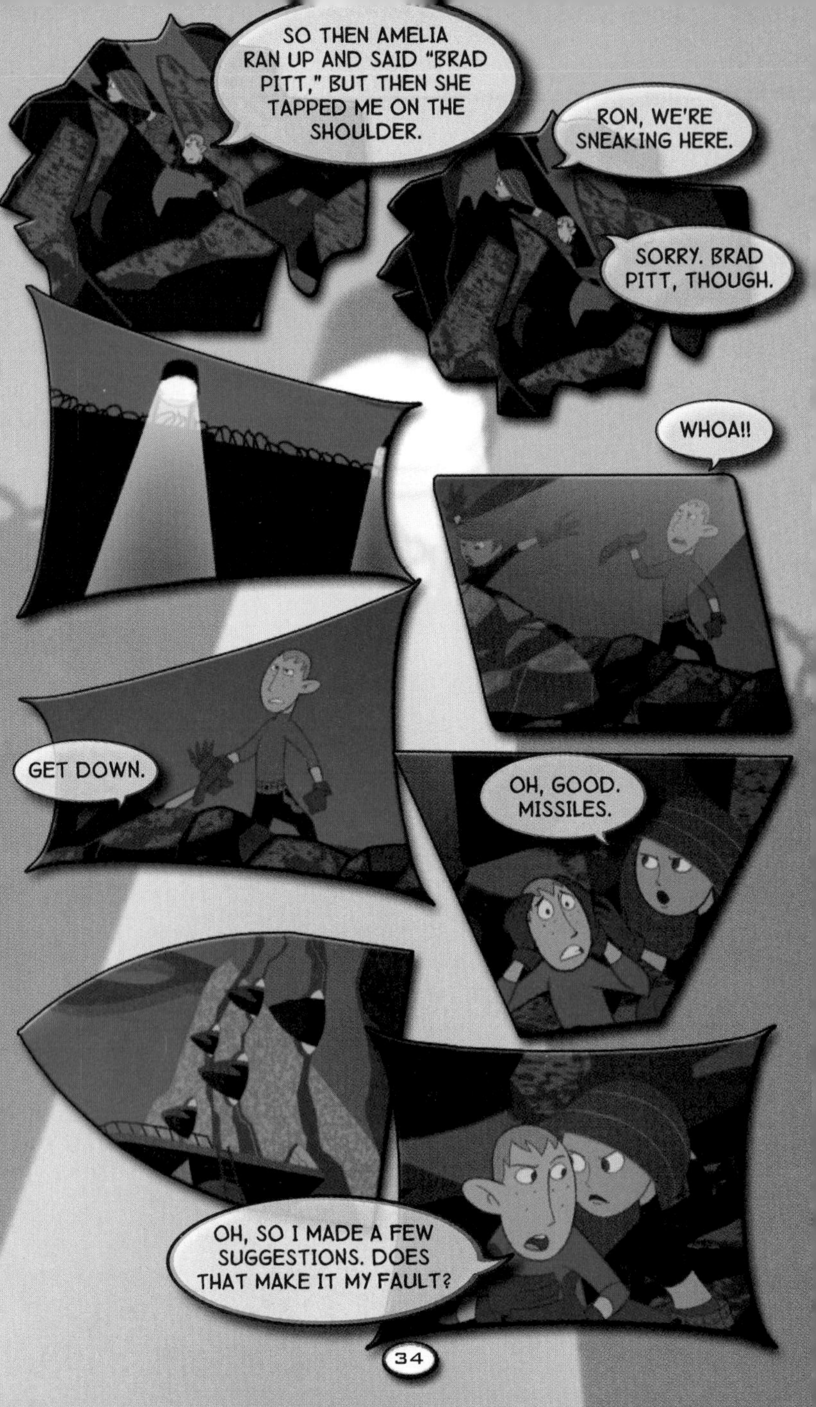
SO THEN AMELIA RAN UP AND SAID "BRAD PITT," BUT THEN SHE TAPPED ME ON THE SHOULDER.
RON, WE'RE SNEAKING HERE.
SORRY. BRAD PITT, THOUGH.
WHOA!!
GET DOWN.
OH, GOOD. MISSILES.
OH, SO I MADE A FEW SUGGESTIONS. DOES THAT MAKE IT MY FAULT?

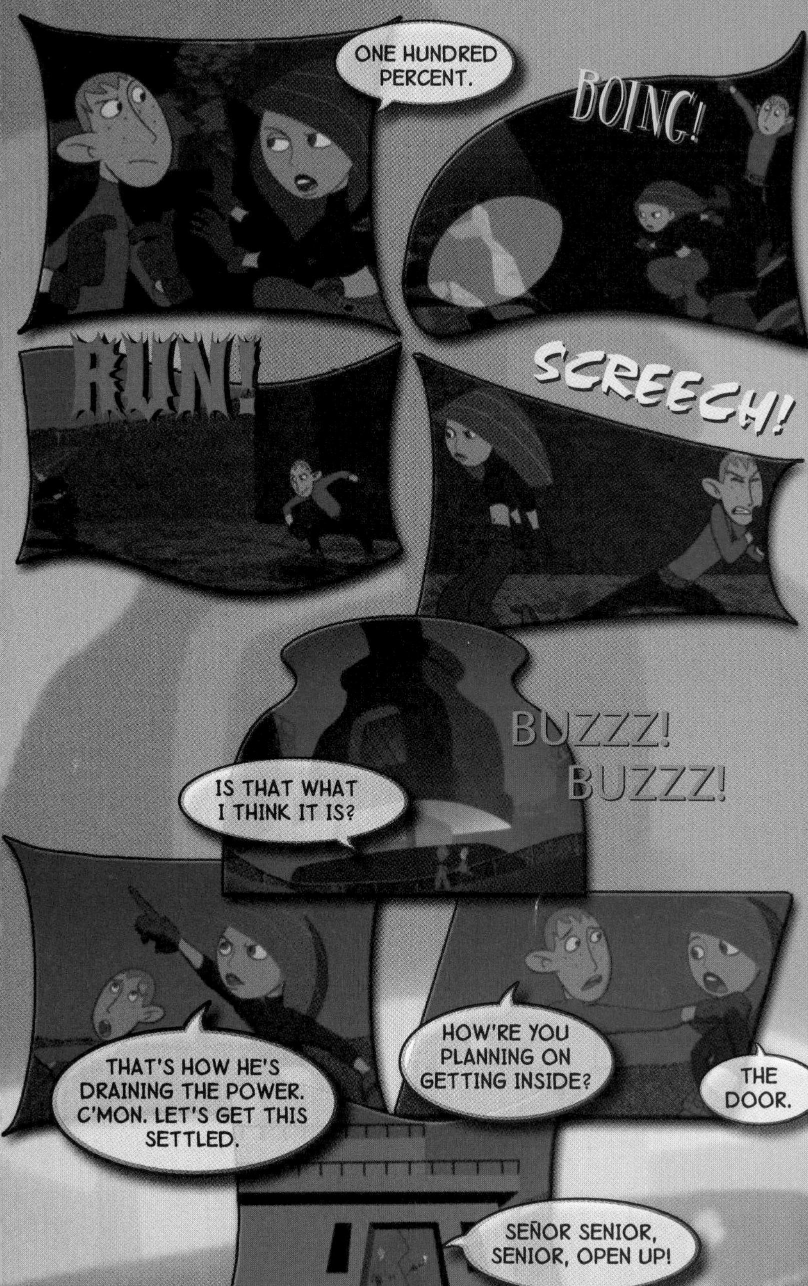
ONE HUNDRED PERCENT.
BOING!
RUN!
SCREECH!
BUZZZ! BUZZZ!
IS THAT WHAT I THINK IT IS?
THAT'S HOW HE'S DRAINING THE POWER. C'MON. LET'S GET THIS SETTLED.
HOW'RE YOU PLANNING ON GETTING INSIDE?
THE DOOR.
SEÑOR SENIOR, SENIOR, OPEN UP!

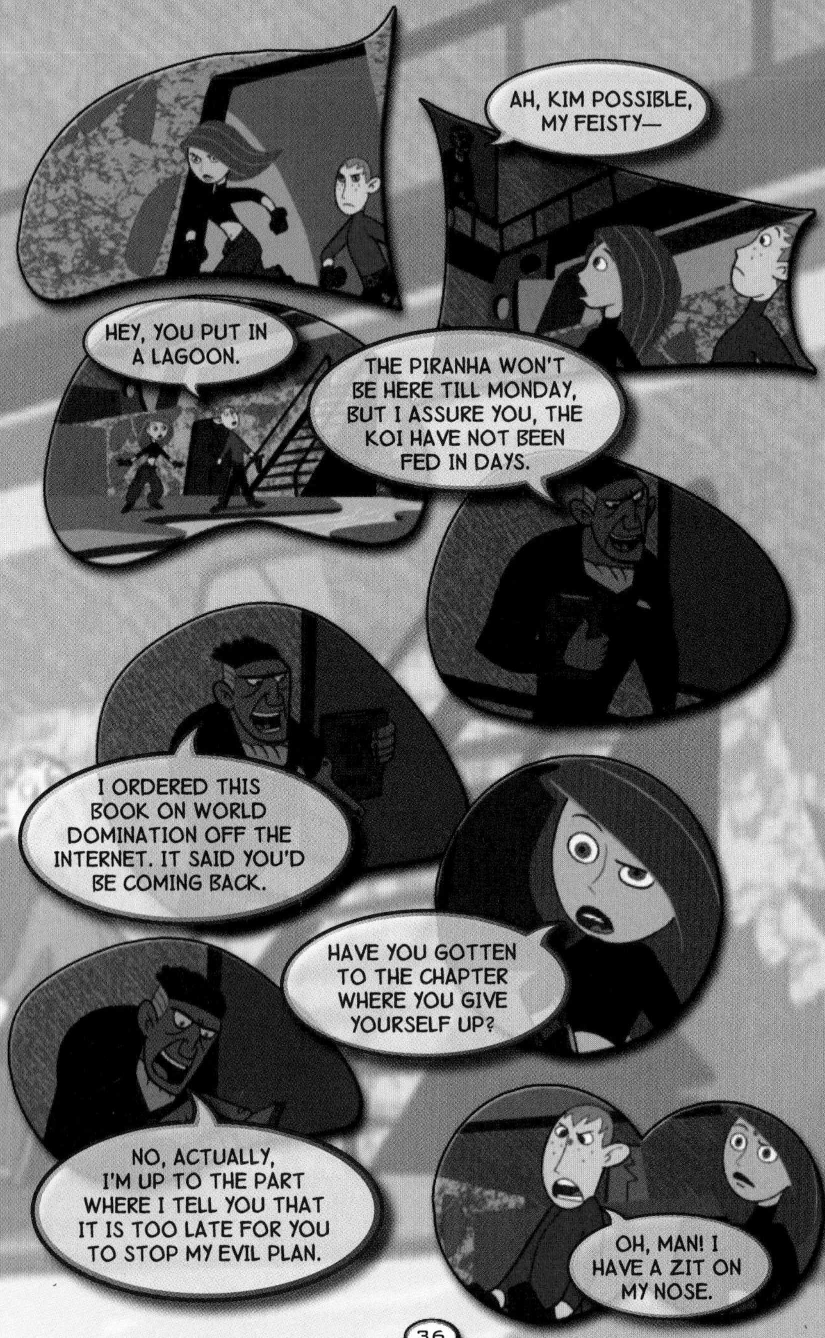
AH, KIM POSSIBLE, MY FEISTY—
HEY, YOU PUT IN A LAGOON.
THE PIRANHA WON'T BE HERE TILL MONDAY, BUT I ASSURE YOU, THE KOI HAVE NOT BEEN FED IN DAYS.
I ORDERED THIS BOOK ON WORLD DOMINATION OFF THE INTERNET. IT SAID YOU'D BE COMING BACK.
HAVE YOU GOTTEN TO THE CHAPTER WHERE YOU GIVE YOURSELF UP?
NO, ACTUALLY, I'M UP TO THE PART WHERE I TELL YOU THAT IT IS TOO LATE FOR YOU TO STOP MY EVIL PLAN.
OH, MAN! I HAVE A ZIT ON MY NOSE.

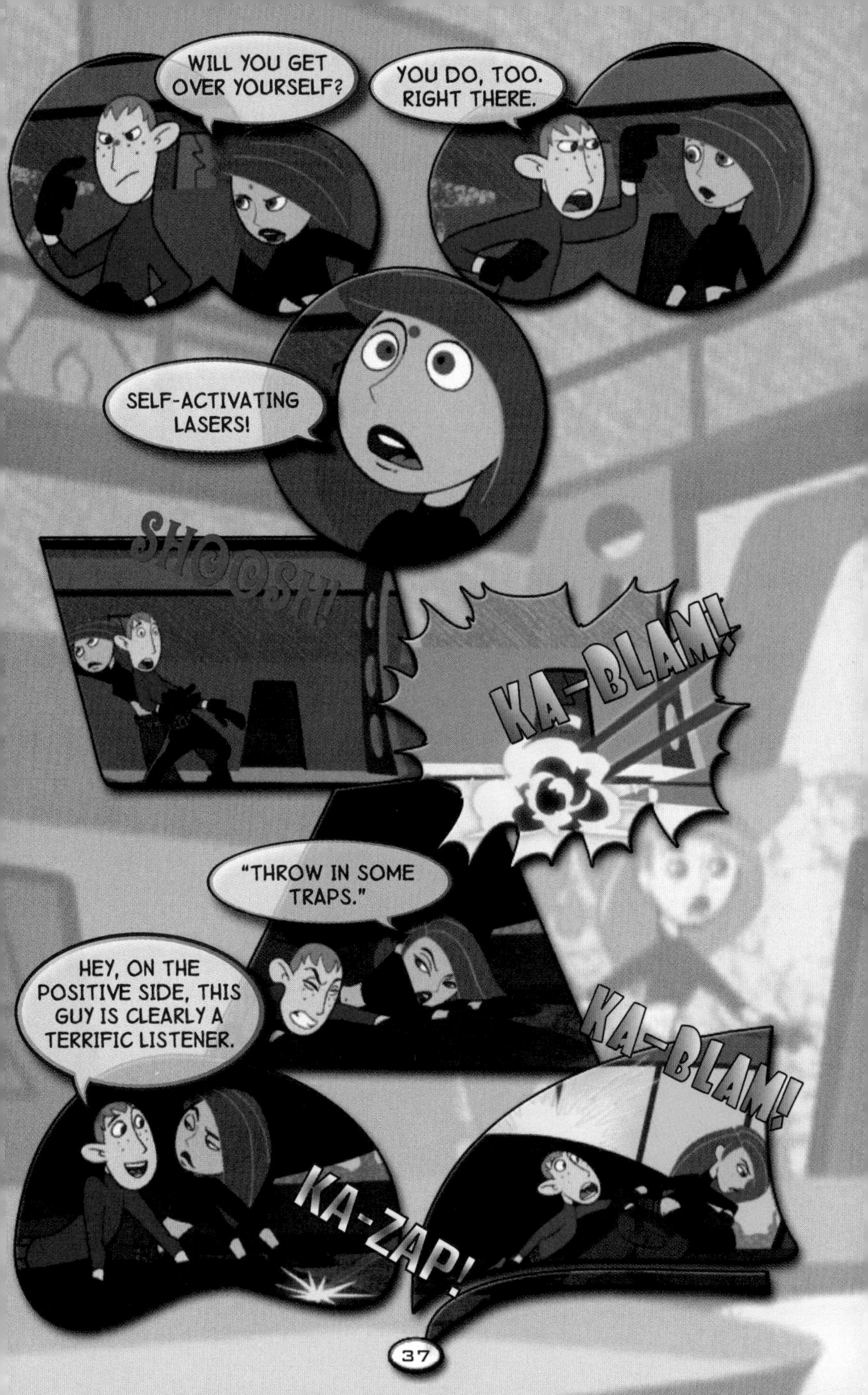
WILL YOU GET OVER YOURSELF?
YOU DO, TOO. RIGHT THERE.
SELF-ACTIVATING LASERS!
SHOOSH!
KA-BLAM!
"THROW IN SOME TRAPS."
HEY, ON THE POSITIVE SIDE, THIS GUY IS CLEARLY A TERRIFIC LISTENER.
KA-ZAP!
KA-BLAM!

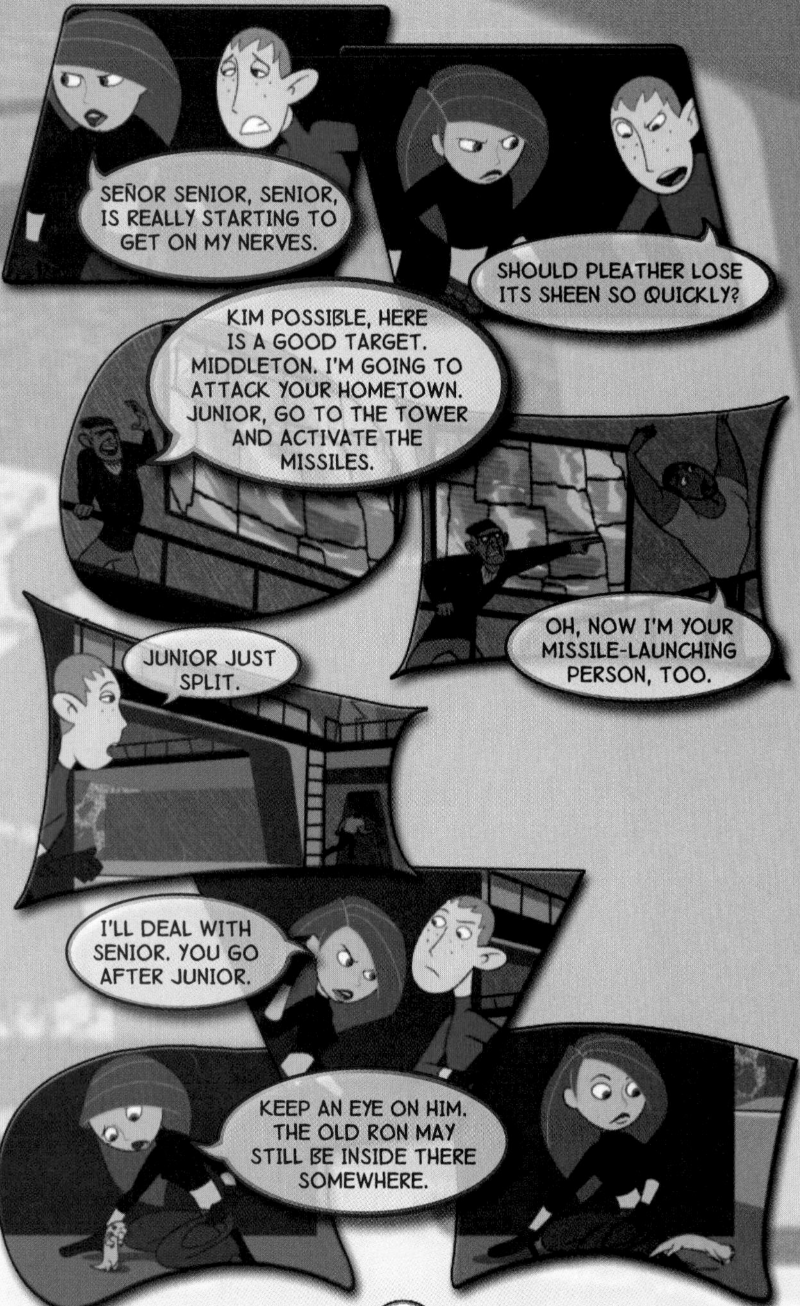
SEÑOR SENIOR, SENIOR, IS REALLY STARTING TO GET ON MY NERVES.
SHOULD PLEATHER LOSE ITS SHEEN SO QUICKLY?
KIM POSSIBLE, HERE IS A GOOD TARGET. MIDDLETON. I'M GOING TO ATTACK YOUR HOMETOWN. JUNIOR, GO TO THE TOWER AND ACTIVATE THE MISSILES.
OH, NOW I'M YOUR MISSILE-LAUNCHING PERSON, TOO.
JUNIOR JUST SPLIT.
I'LL DEAL WITH SENIOR. YOU GO AFTER JUNIOR.
KEEP AN EYE ON HIM. THE OLD RON MAY STILL BE INSIDE THERE SOMEWHERE.

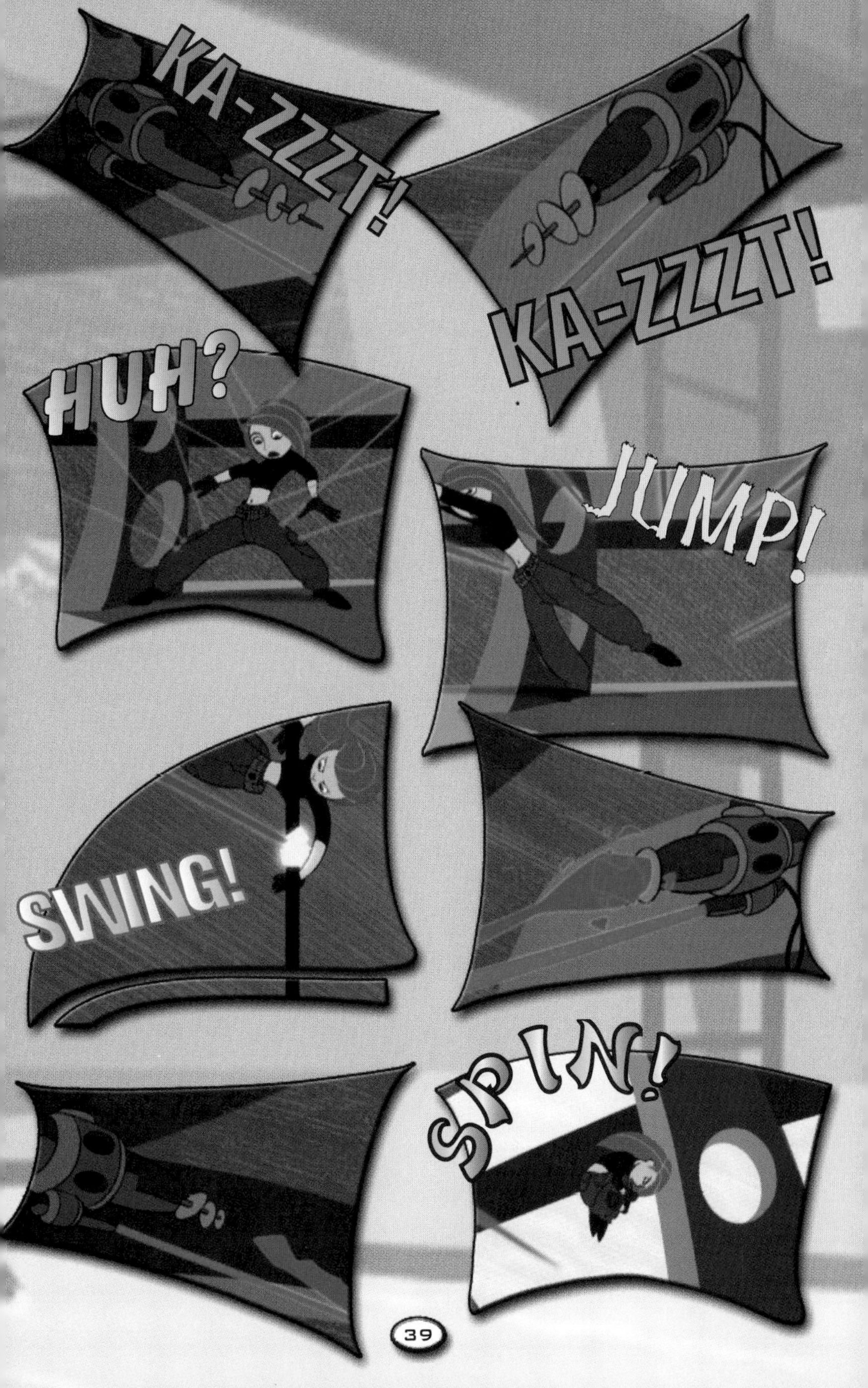
KA-ZZZZT!
KA-ZZZZT!
HUH?
JUMP!
SWING!
SPIN!

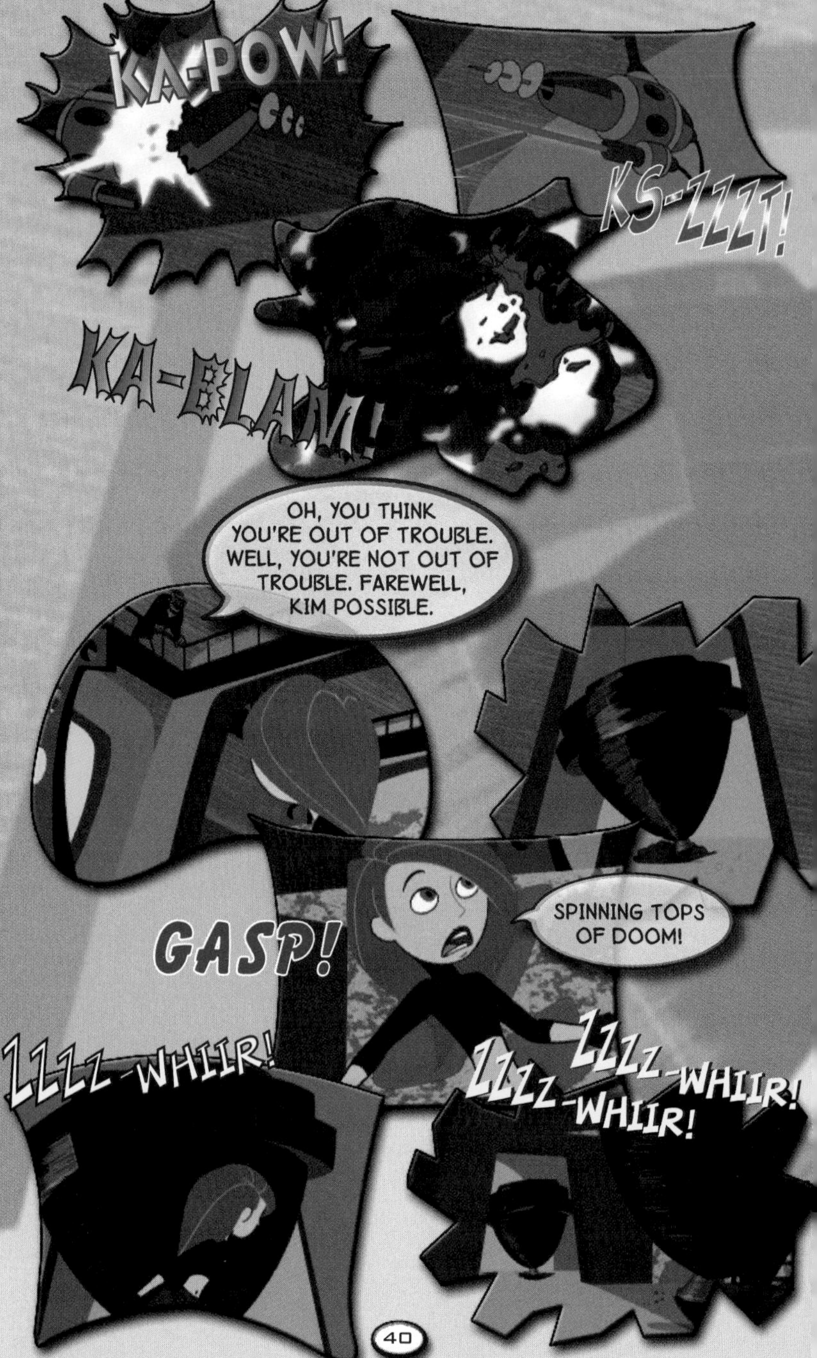
KA-POW!
KS-ZZZT!
KA-BLAM!
OH, YOU THINK YOU'RE OUT OF TROUBLE. WELL, YOU'RE NOT OUT OF TROUBLE. FAREWELL, KIM POSSIBLE.
GASP!
SPINNING TOPS OF DOOM!
ZZZZ-WHIIR!
ZZZZ-WHIIR!
ZZZZ-WHIIR!

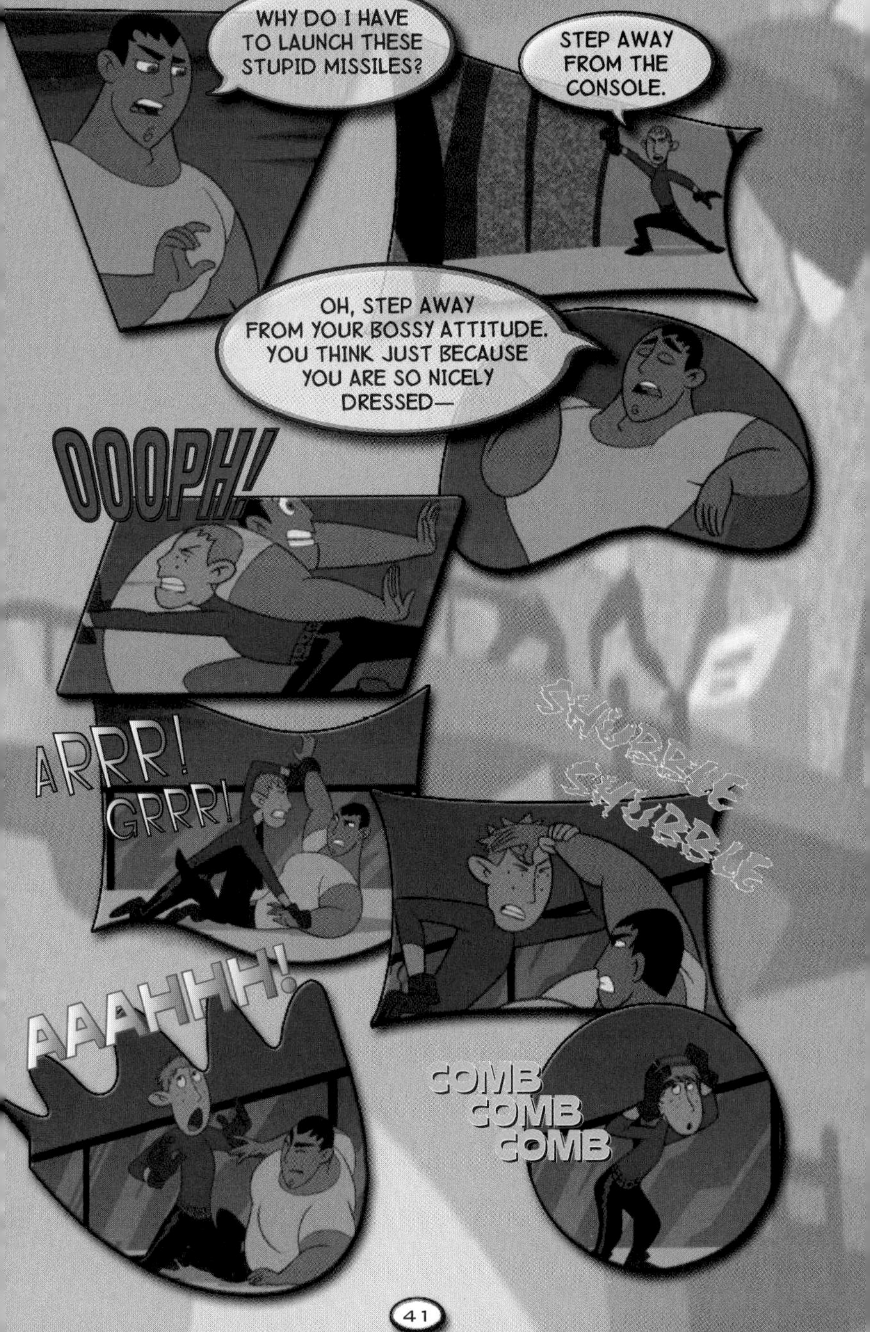
WHY DO I HAVE TO LAUNCH THESE STUPID MISSILES?
STEP AWAY FROM THE CONSOLE.
OH, STEP AWAY FROM YOUR BOSSY ATTITUDE. YOU THINK JUST BECAUSE YOU ARE SO NICELY DRESSED—
OOOPH!
ARRRR!
GRRRR!
COMB
COMB
COMB

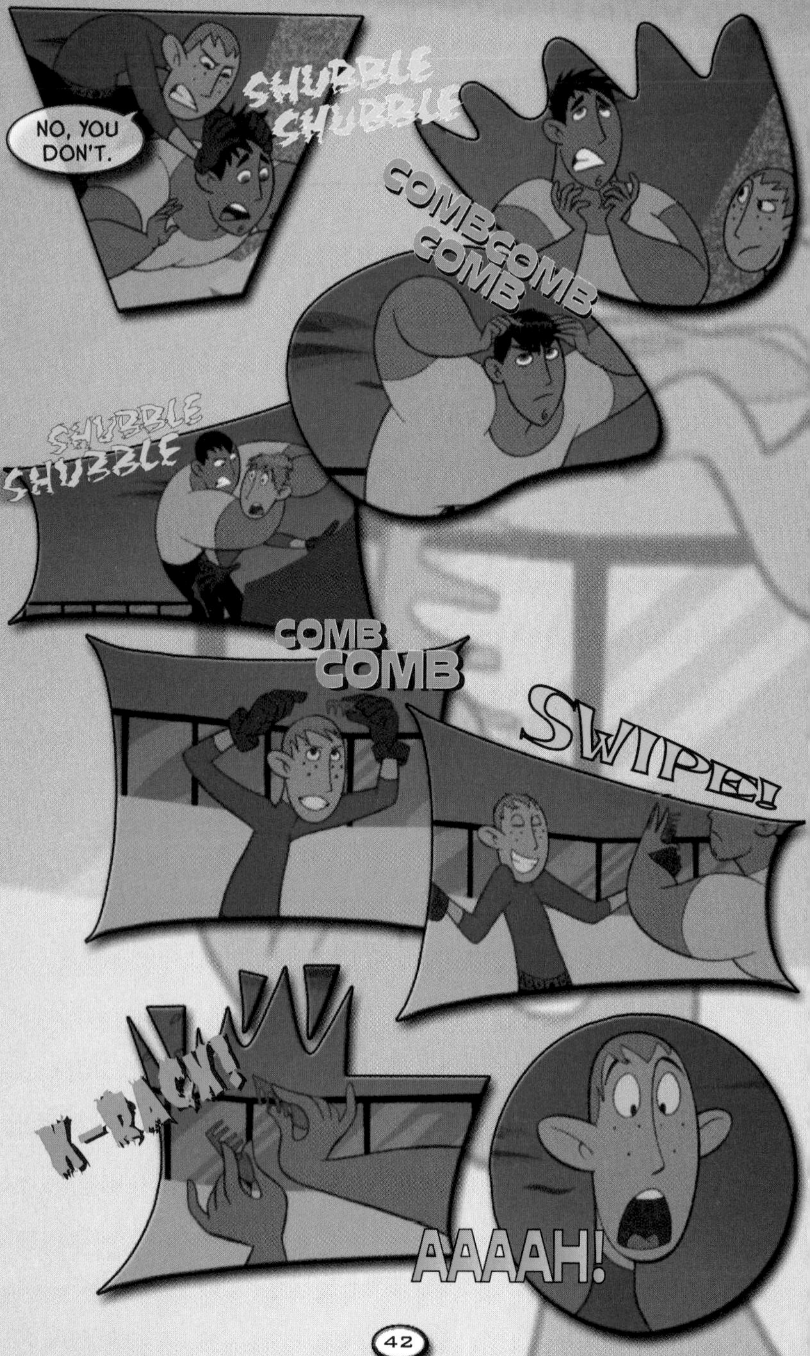
NO, YOU DON'T.
SHUBBLE SHUBBLE
COMBCOMB COMB
SHUBBLE SHUBBLE
COMB COMB
SWIPE!
K-RACK!
AAAAH!

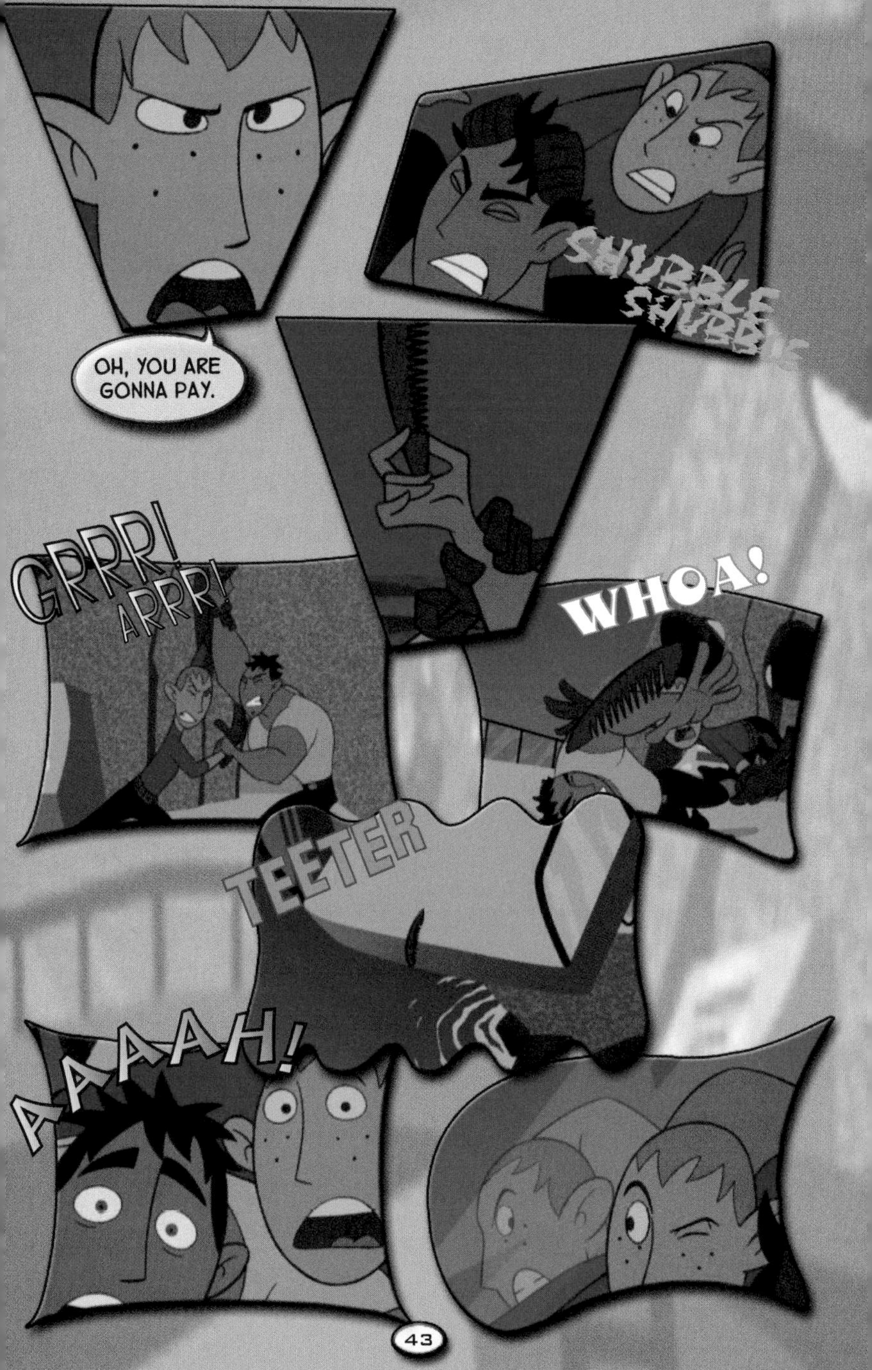
OH, YOU ARE GONNA PAY.
SHUBBLE SHUBBLE
GRRR! ARRR!
WHOA!
TEETER
AAAAAH!

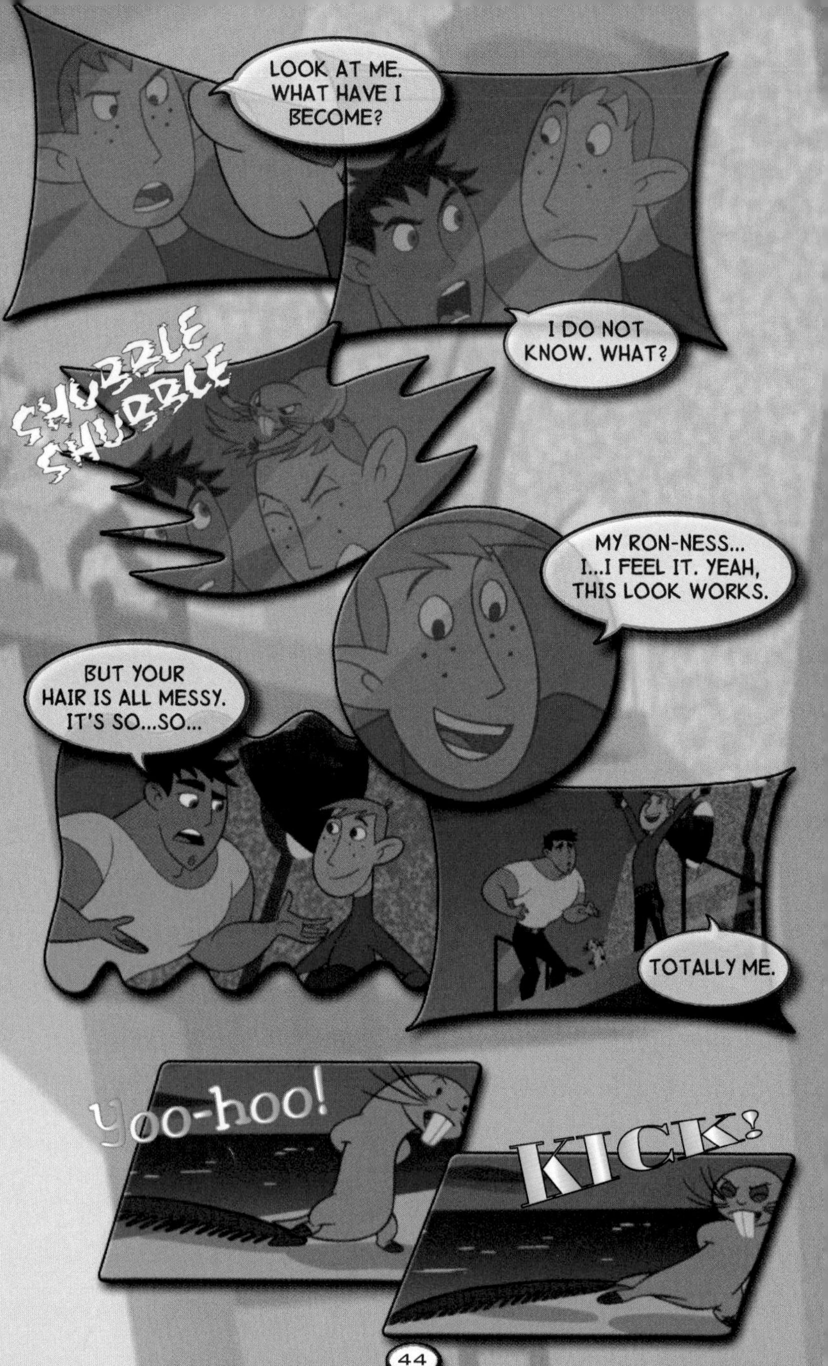
LOOK AT ME. WHAT HAVE I BECOME?
I DO NOT KNOW. WHAT?
SHUBBLE SHUBBLE
MY RON-NESS... I...I FEEL IT. YEAH, THIS LOOK WORKS.
BUT YOUR HAIR IS ALL MESSY. IT'S SO...SO...
TOTALLY ME.
yoo-hoo!
KICK!

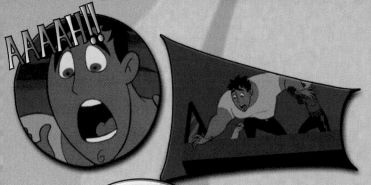

AAAAH!!

WHOA! THE STAIRS. USE THE STAIRS.

WHOOSH!

BEEP! BEEP!

WHOOSH!

CLUNCK!

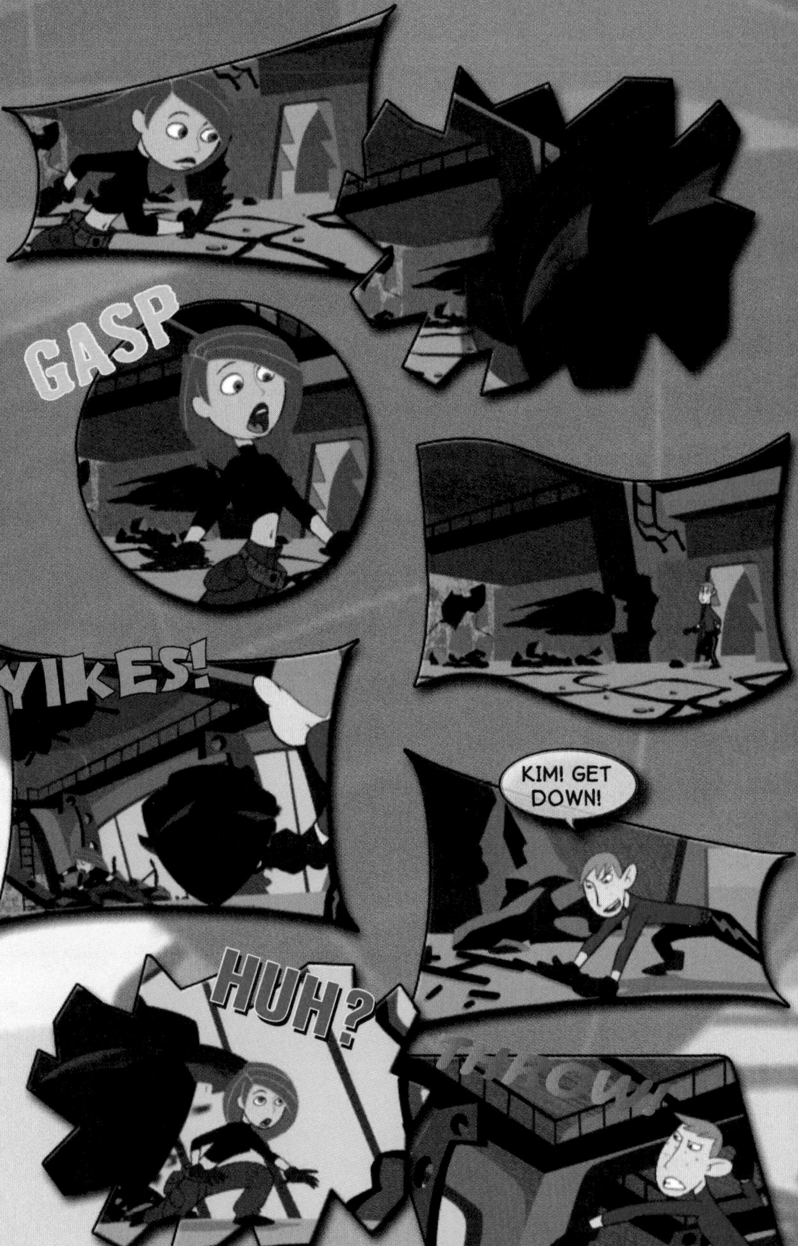
GASP
YIKES!
KIM! GET DOWN!
HUH?

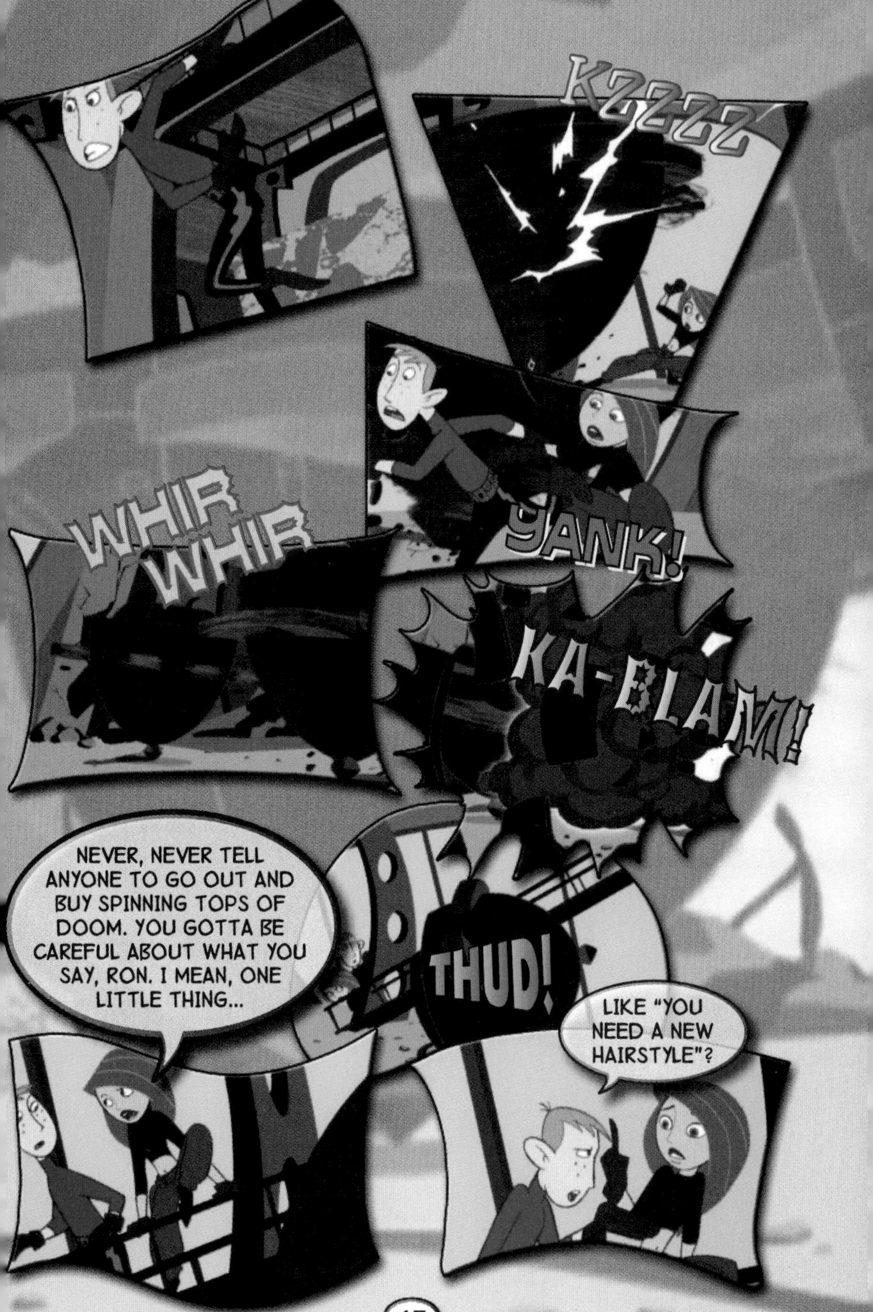
KZZZZ
WHIR WHIR
YANK!
KA-BLAM!
THUD!
NEVER, NEVER TELL ANYONE TO GO OUT AND BUY SPINNING TOPS OF DOOM. YOU GOTTA BE CAREFUL ABOUT WHAT YOU SAY, RON. I MEAN, ONE LITTLE THING...
LIKE "YOU NEED A NEW HAIRSTYLE"?

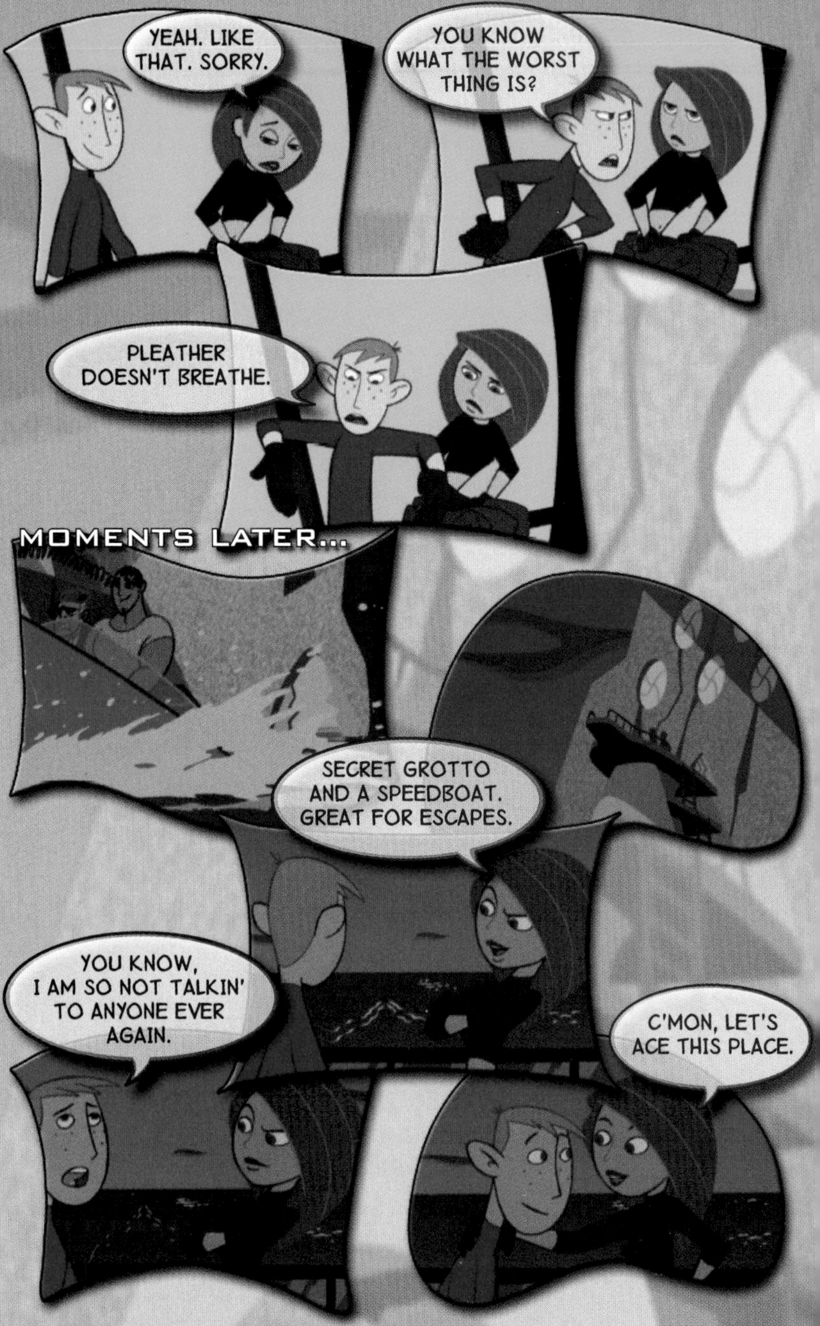
YEAH. LIKE THAT. SORRY.
YOU KNOW WHAT THE WORST THING IS?
PLEATHER DOESN'T BREATHE.
MOMENTS LATER...
SECRET GROTTO AND A SPEEDBOAT. GREAT FOR ESCAPES.
YOU KNOW, I AM SO NOT TALKIN' TO ANYONE EVER AGAIN.
C'MON, LET'S ACE THIS PLACE.

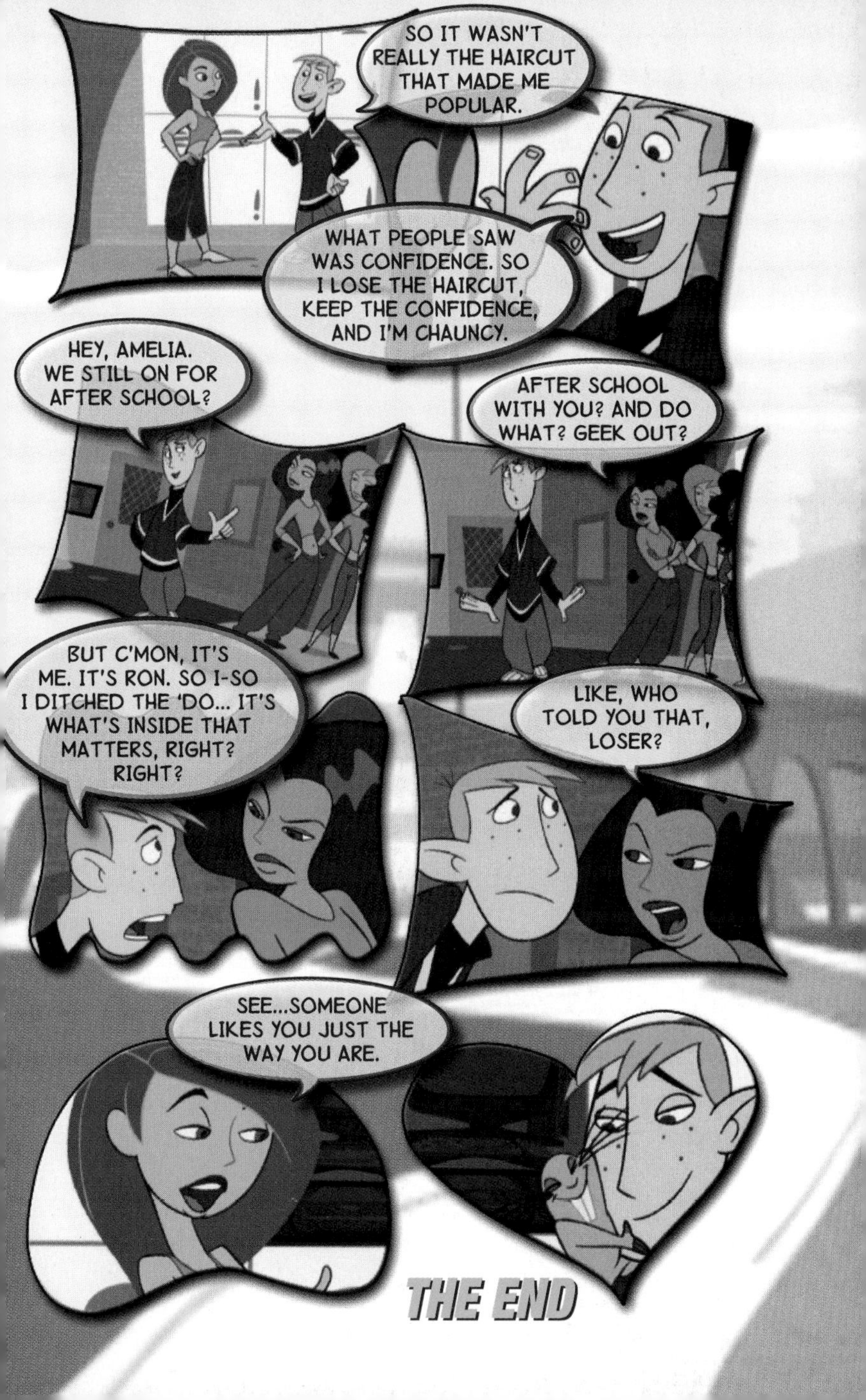
SO IT WASN'T REALLY THE HAIRCUT THAT MADE ME POPULAR.
WHAT PEOPLE SAW WAS CONFIDENCE. SO I LOSE THE HAIRCUT, KEEP THE CONFIDENCE, AND I'M CHAUNCY.
HEY, AMELIA. WE STILL ON FOR AFTER SCHOOL?
AFTER SCHOOL WITH YOU? AND DO WHAT? GEEK OUT?
BUT C'MON, IT'S ME. IT'S RON. SO I-SO I DITCHED THE 'DO... IT'S WHAT'S INSIDE THAT MATTERS, RIGHT? RIGHT?
LIKE, WHO TOLD YOU THAT, LOSER?
SEE...SOMEONE LIKES YOU JUST THE WAY YOU ARE.
THE END

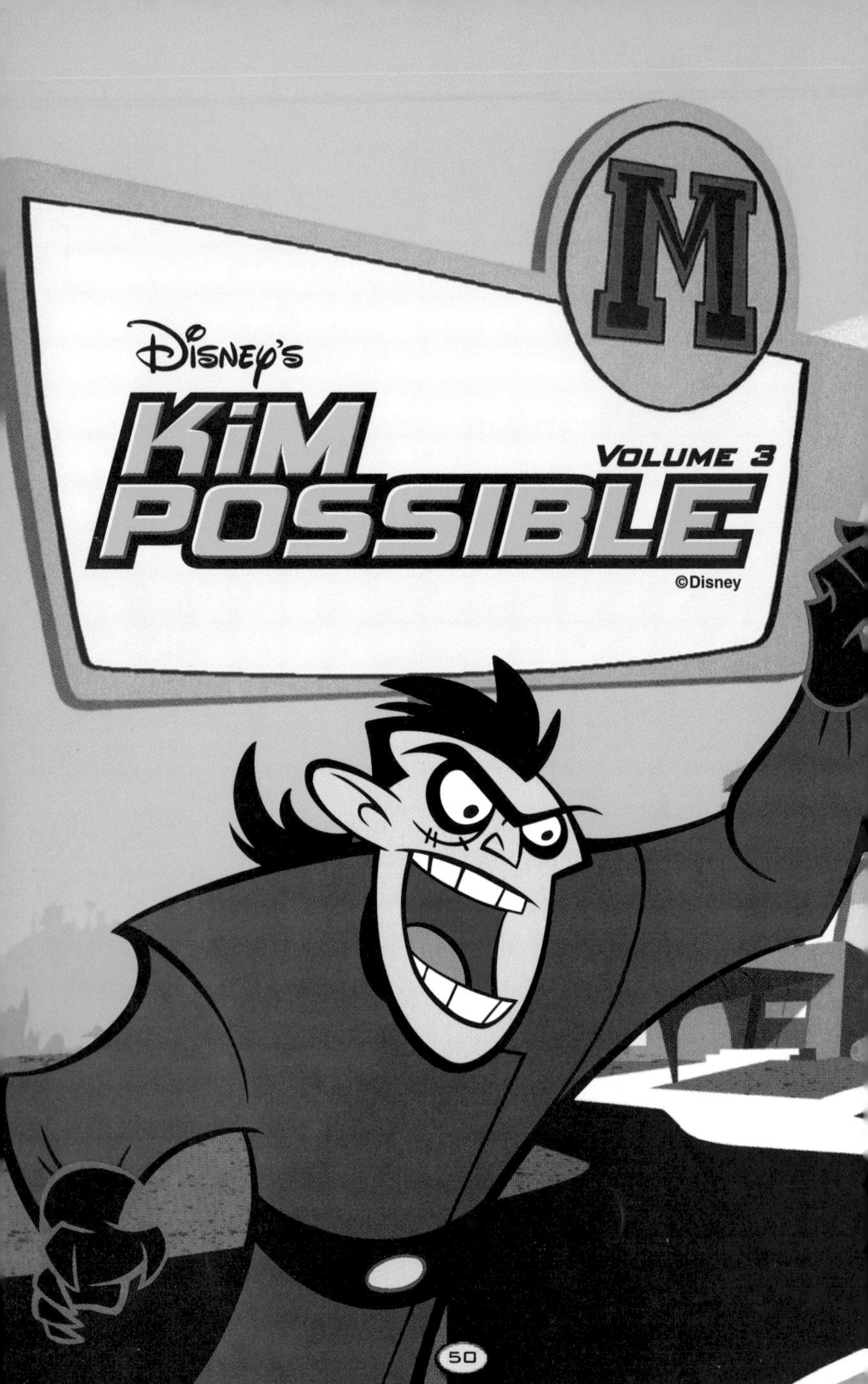
M
Disney's
Kim Possible
Volume 3
©Disney

EPISODE 6: MIND GAMES

IN YET ANOTHER SINISTER PLAY FOR WORLD DOMINATION, DRAKKEN AND SHEGO STEAL A TOP-SECRET GOVERNMENT WEAPON. KIM AND RON ARE HOT ON HIS TRAIL WHEN A BRAIN-SWITCHING MACHINE ACCIDENTALLY TRAPS KIM IN RON'S BODY—AND VICE VERSA. HOW WILL THE POWER DUO SAVE THE WORLD WHEN THEY CAN'T EVEN GET THROUGH THE SCHOOL DAY?

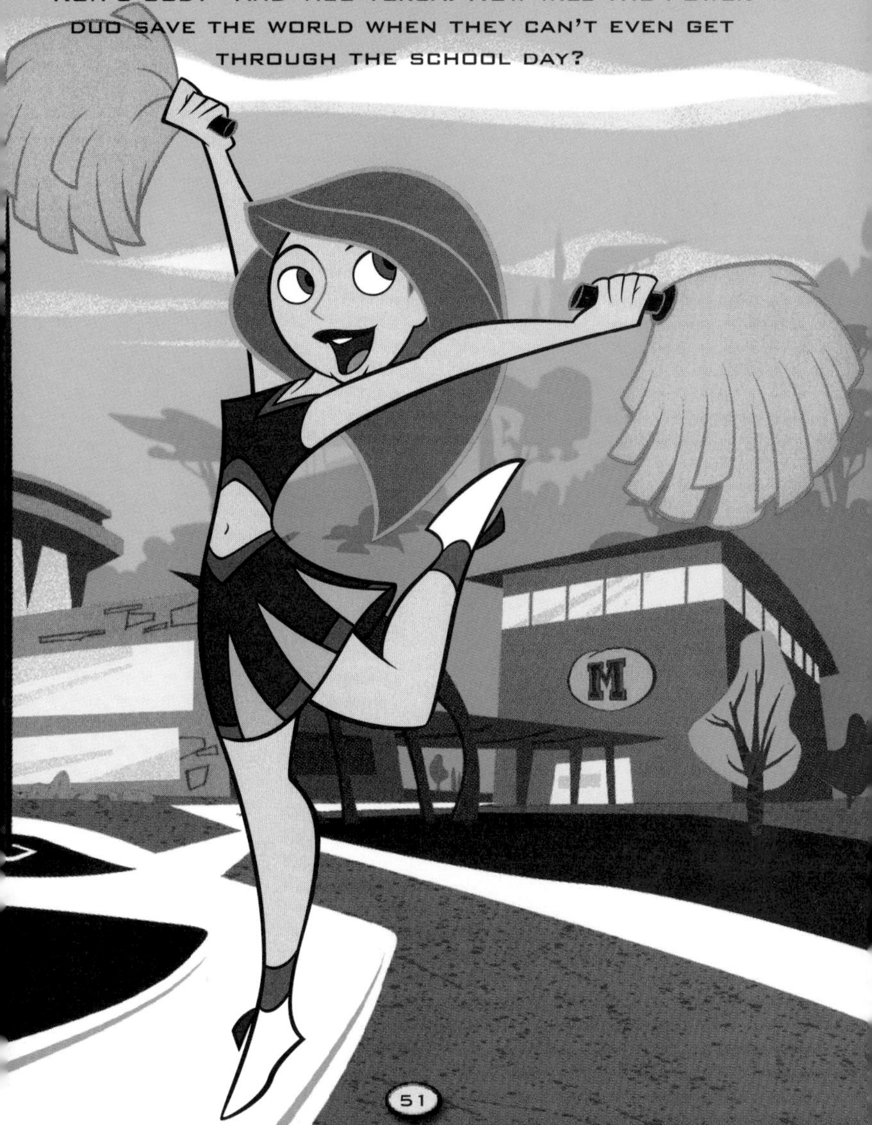

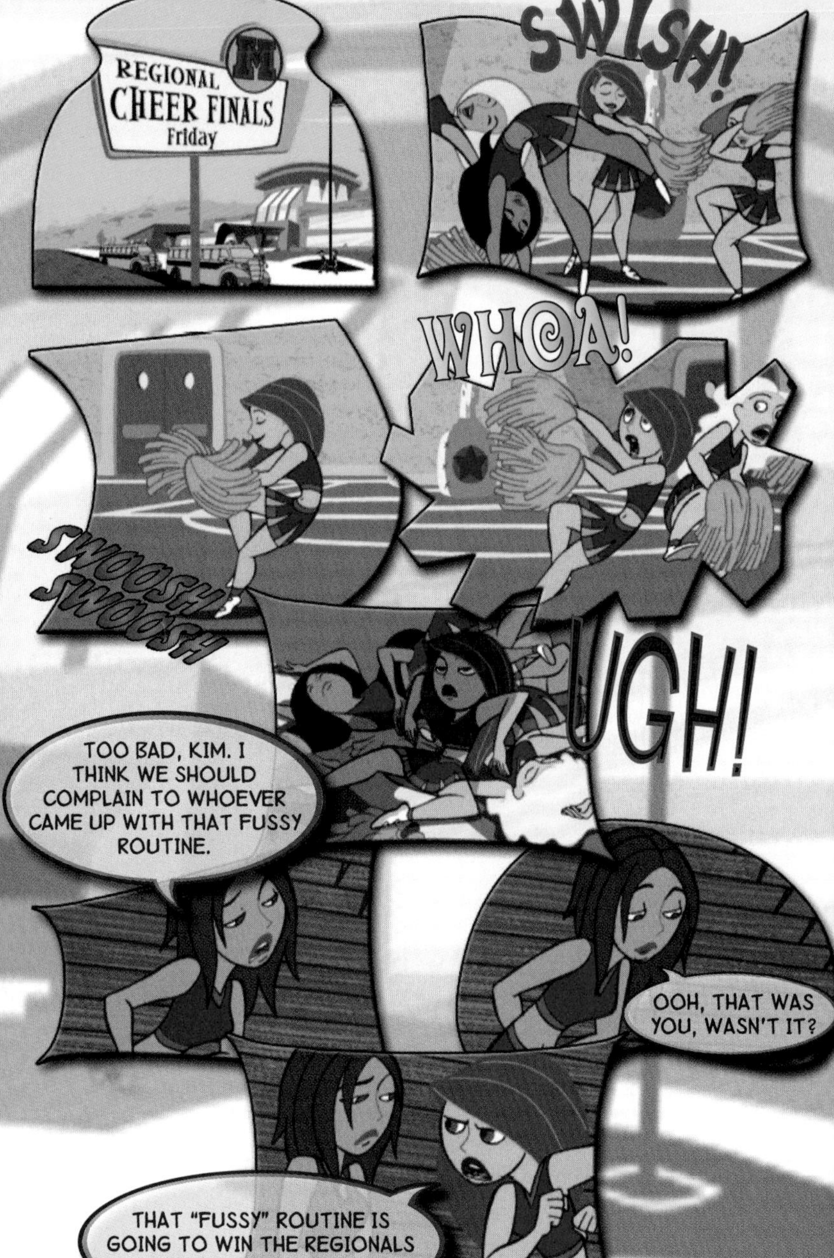
REGIONAL
CHEER FINALS
Friday
SWISH!
WHOA!
SWOOSH!
SWOOSH
UGH!
TOO BAD, KIM. I THINK WE SHOULD COMPLAIN TO WHOEVER CAME UP WITH THAT FUSSY ROUTINE.
OOH, THAT WAS YOU, WASN'T IT?
THAT "FUSSY" ROUTINE IS GOING TO WIN THE REGIONALS TOMORROW, BONNIE...

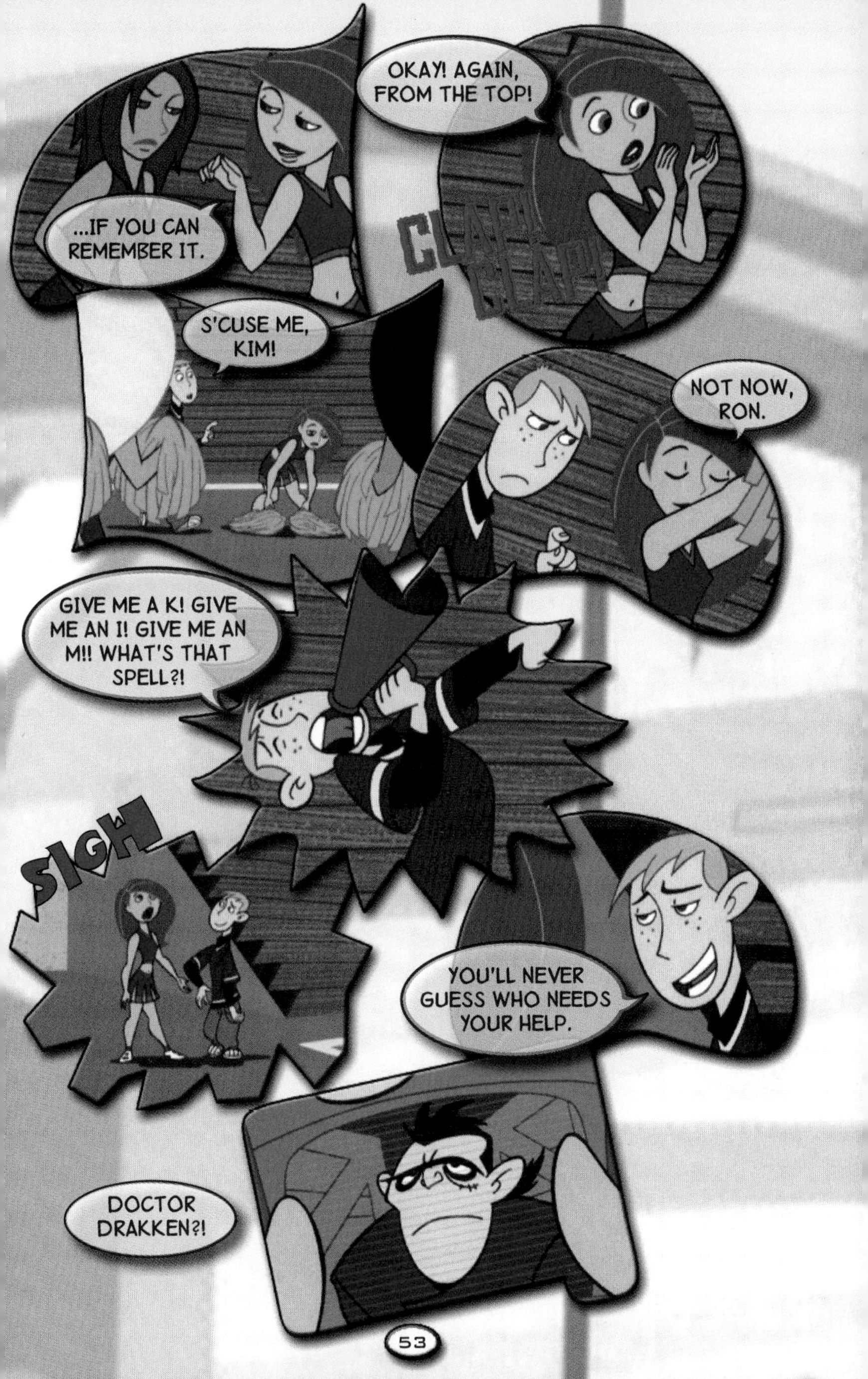
...IF YOU CAN REMEMBER IT.
OKAY! AGAIN, FROM THE TOP!
CLAP! CLAP!
S'CUSE ME, KIM!
NOT NOW, RON.
GIVE ME A K! GIVE ME AN I! GIVE ME AN M!! WHAT'S THAT SPELL?!
SIGH
YOU'LL NEVER GUESS WHO NEEDS YOUR HELP.
DOCTOR DRAKKEN?!

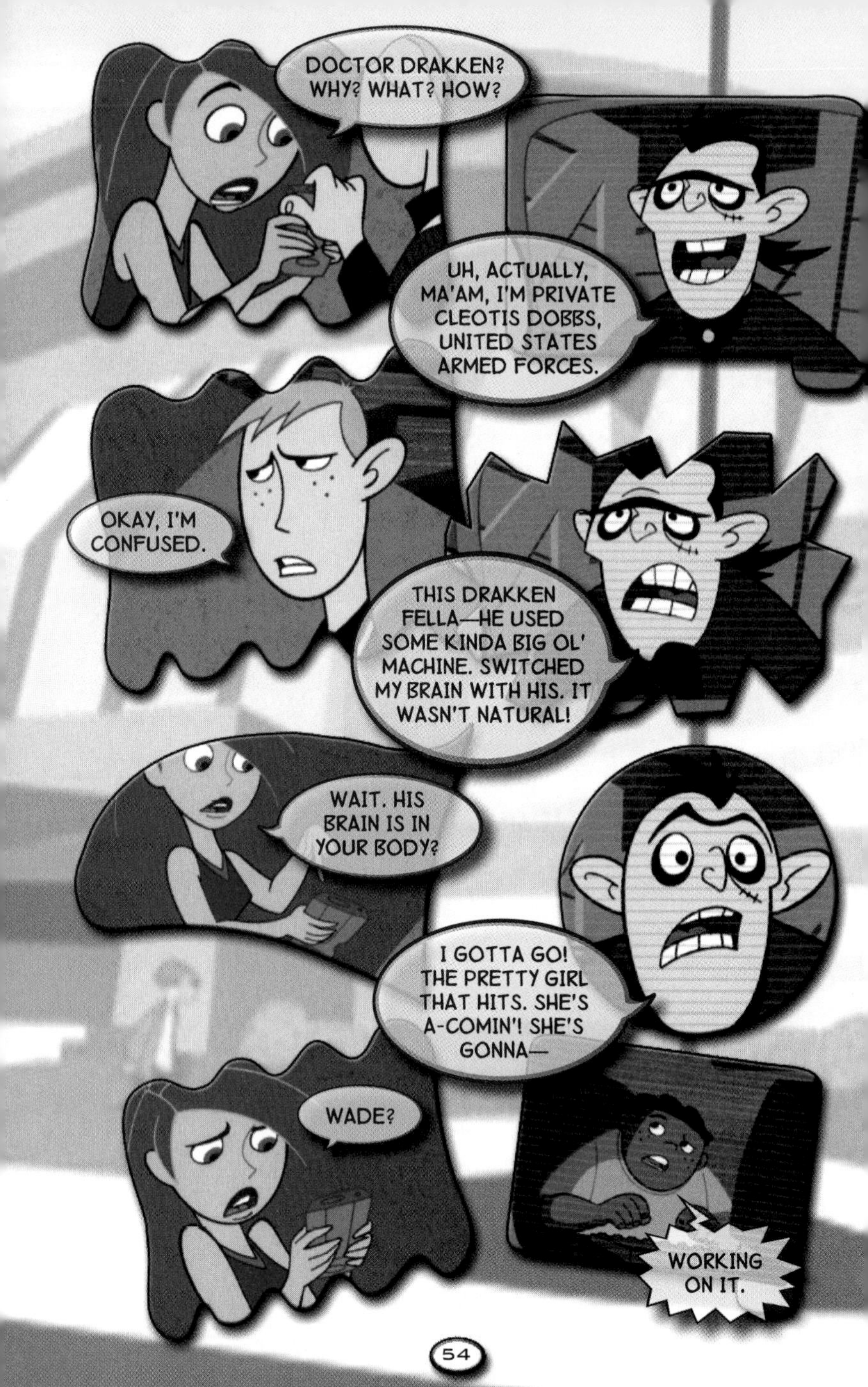
DOCTOR DRAKKEN? WHY? WHAT? HOW?
UH, ACTUALLY, MA'AM, I'M PRIVATE CLEOTIS DOBBS, UNITED STATES ARMED FORCES.
OKAY, I'M CONFUSED.
THIS DRAKKEN FELLA—HE USED SOME KINDA BIG OL' MACHINE. SWITCHED MY BRAIN WITH HIS. IT WASN'T NATURAL!
WAIT. HIS BRAIN IS IN YOUR BODY?
I GOTTA GO! THE PRETTY GIRL THAT HITS. SHE'S A-COMIN'! SHE'S GONNA—
WADE?
WORKING ON IT.

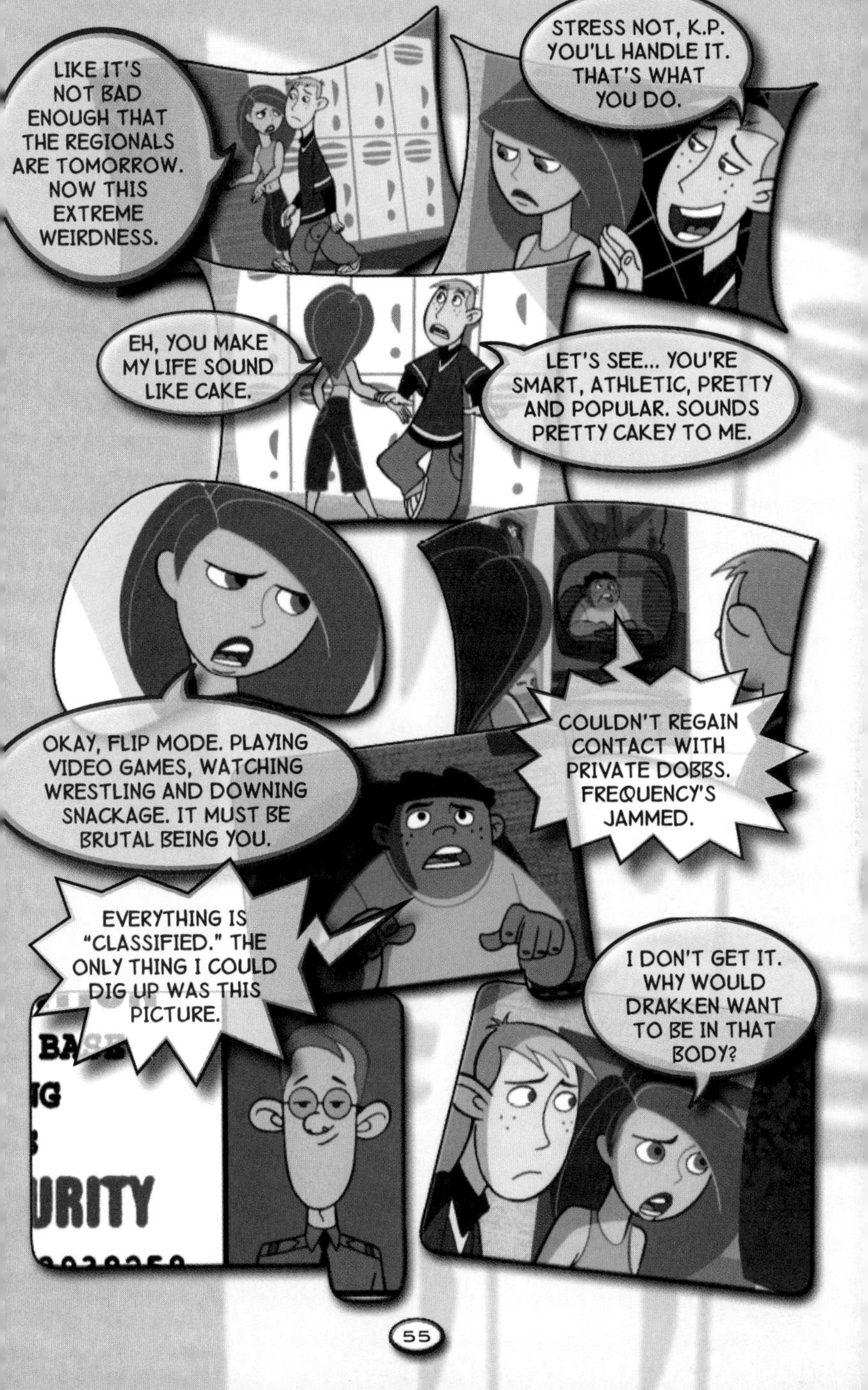
LIKE IT'S NOT BAD ENOUGH THAT THE REGIONALS ARE TOMORROW. NOW THIS EXTREME WEIRDNESS.
STRESS NOT, K.P. YOU'LL HANDLE IT. THAT'S WHAT YOU DO.
EH, YOU MAKE MY LIFE SOUND LIKE CAKE.
LET'S SEE... YOU'RE SMART, ATHLETIC, PRETTY AND POPULAR. SOUNDS PRETTY CAKEY TO ME.
OKAY, FLIP MODE. PLAYING VIDEO GAMES, WATCHING WRESTLING AND DOWNING SNACKAGE. IT MUST BE BRUTAL BEING YOU.
COULDN'T REGAIN CONTACT WITH PRIVATE DOBBS. FREQUENCY'S JAMMED.
EVERYTHING IS "CLASSIFIED." THE ONLY THING I COULD DIG UP WAS THIS PICTURE.
I DON'T GET IT. WHY WOULD DRAKKEN WANT TO BE IN THAT BODY?

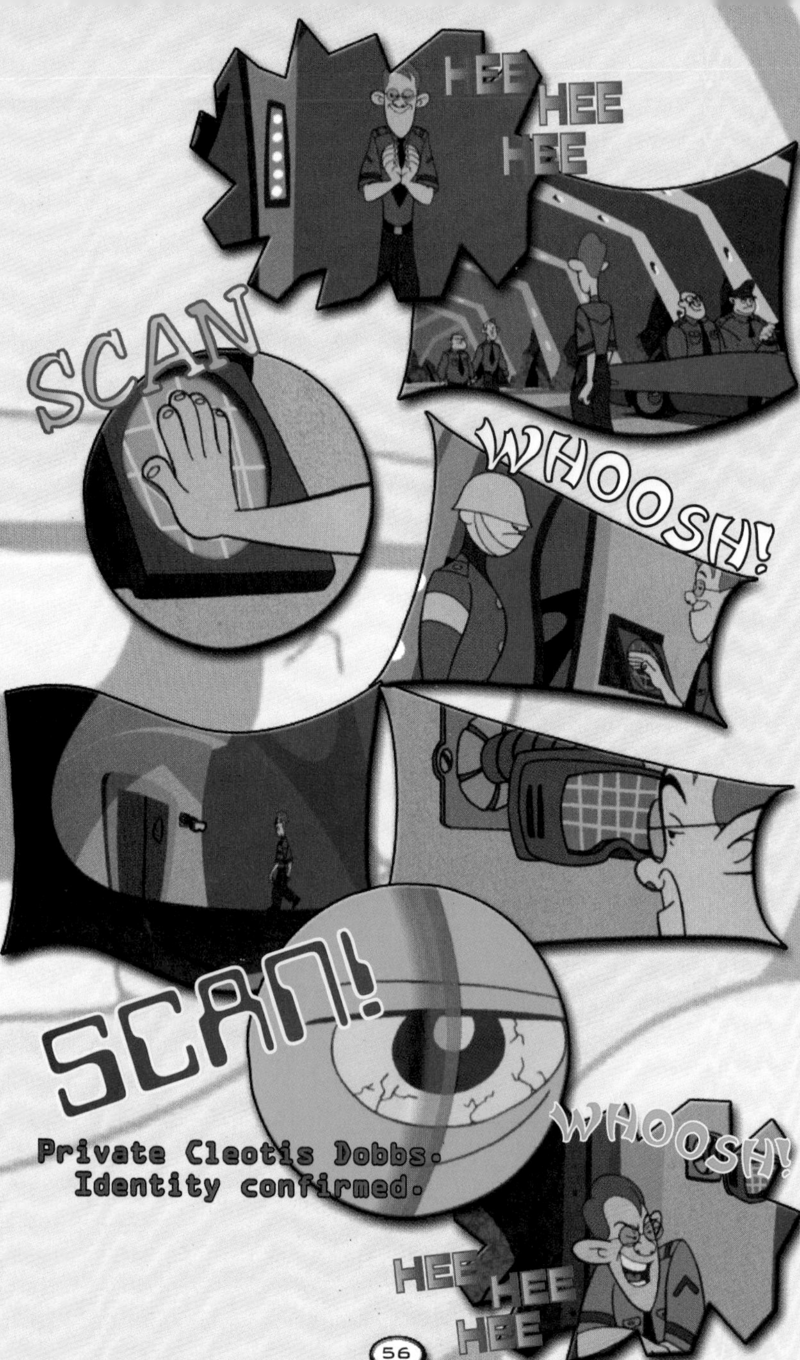

HEE HEE HEE
SCAN
WHOOSH!
SCAN!
Private Cleotis Dobbs.
Identity confirmed.
WHOOSH!
HEE HEE HEE

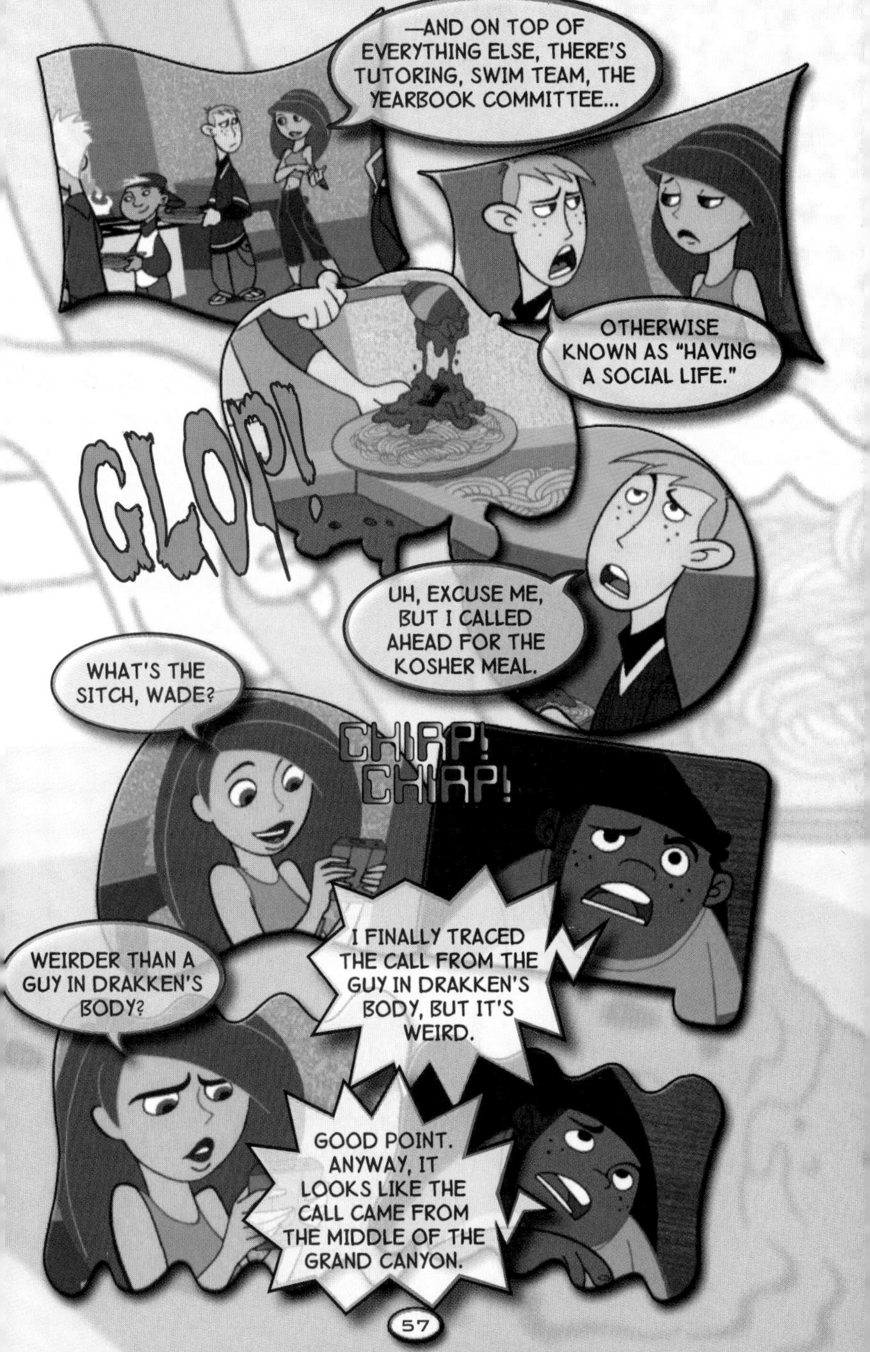
—AND ON TOP OF EVERYTHING ELSE, THERE'S TUTORING, SWIM TEAM, THE YEARBOOK COMMITTEE...
OTHERWISE KNOWN AS "HAVING A SOCIAL LIFE."
GLOP!
UH, EXCUSE ME, BUT I CALLED AHEAD FOR THE KOSHER MEAL.
WHAT'S THE SITCH, WADE?
CHIRP! CHIRP!
I FINALLY TRACED THE CALL FROM THE GUY IN DRAKKEN'S BODY, BUT IT'S WEIRD.
WEIRDER THAN A GUY IN DRAKKEN'S BODY?
GOOD POINT. ANYWAY, IT LOOKS LIKE THE CALL CAME FROM THE MIDDLE OF THE GRAND CANYON.

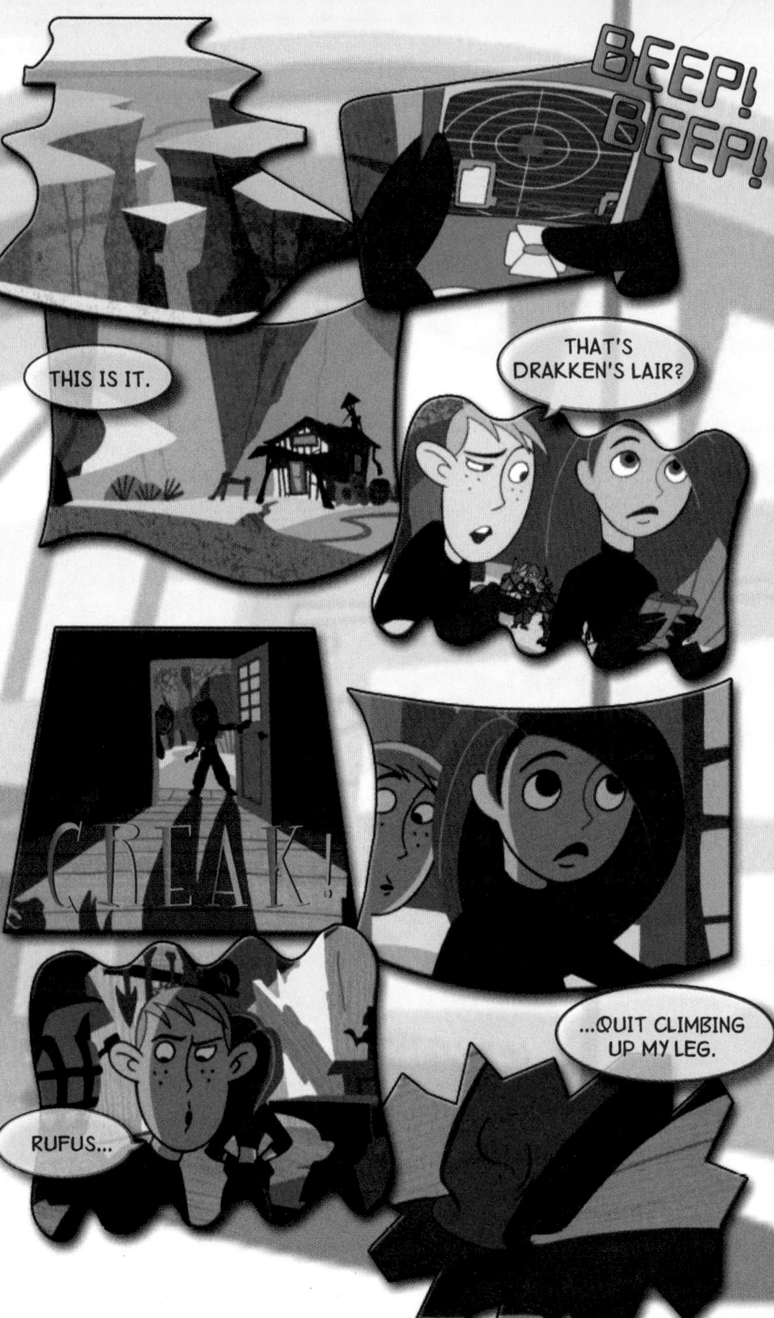
BEEP! BEEP!
THIS IS IT.
THAT'S DRAKKEN'S LAIR?
CREAK!
RUFUS...
...QUIT CLIMBING UP MY LEG.

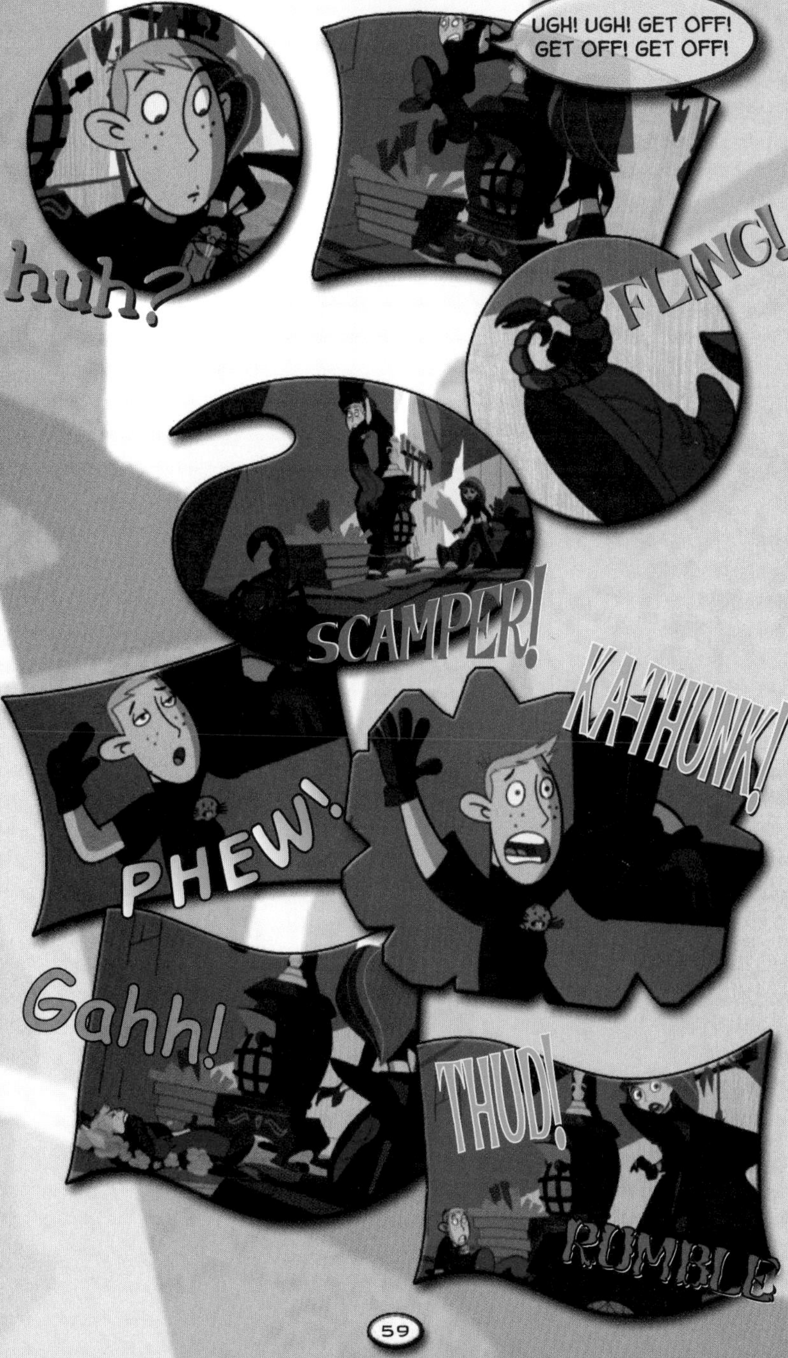
huh?
UGH! UGH! GET OFF! GET OFF! GET OFF!
FLING!
SCAMPER!
PHEW!
KA-THUNK!
Gahh!
THUD!
RUMBLE

CREAK!
MISTER DUMB LUCK.
NOT DUMB LUCK, KIM. DUMB SKILLS.
GOING DOWN
DOWN
DOWN
DOWN
DING!

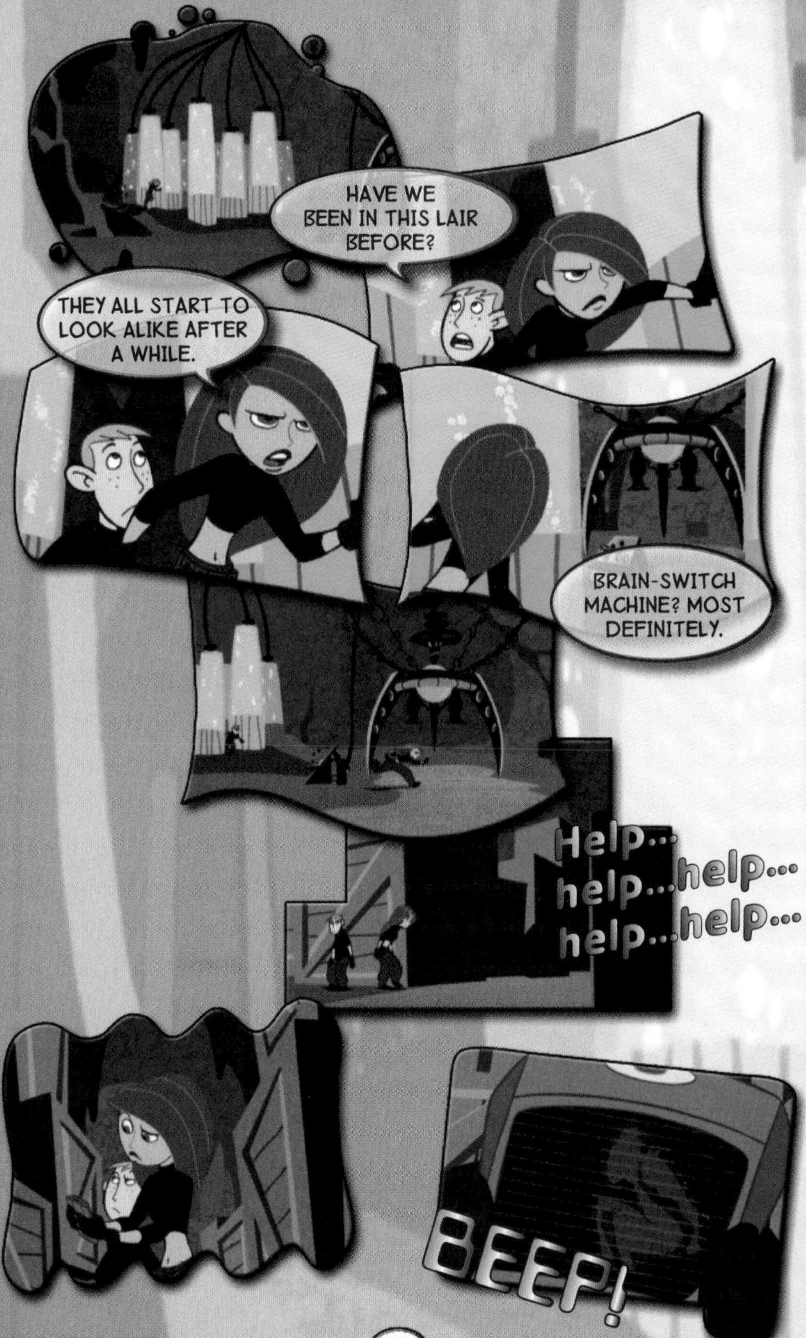
HAVE WE BEEN IN THIS LAIR BEFORE?
THEY ALL START TO LOOK ALIKE AFTER A WHILE.
BRAIN-SWITCH MACHINE? MOST DEFINITELY.
Help... help... help... help... help...
BEEP!

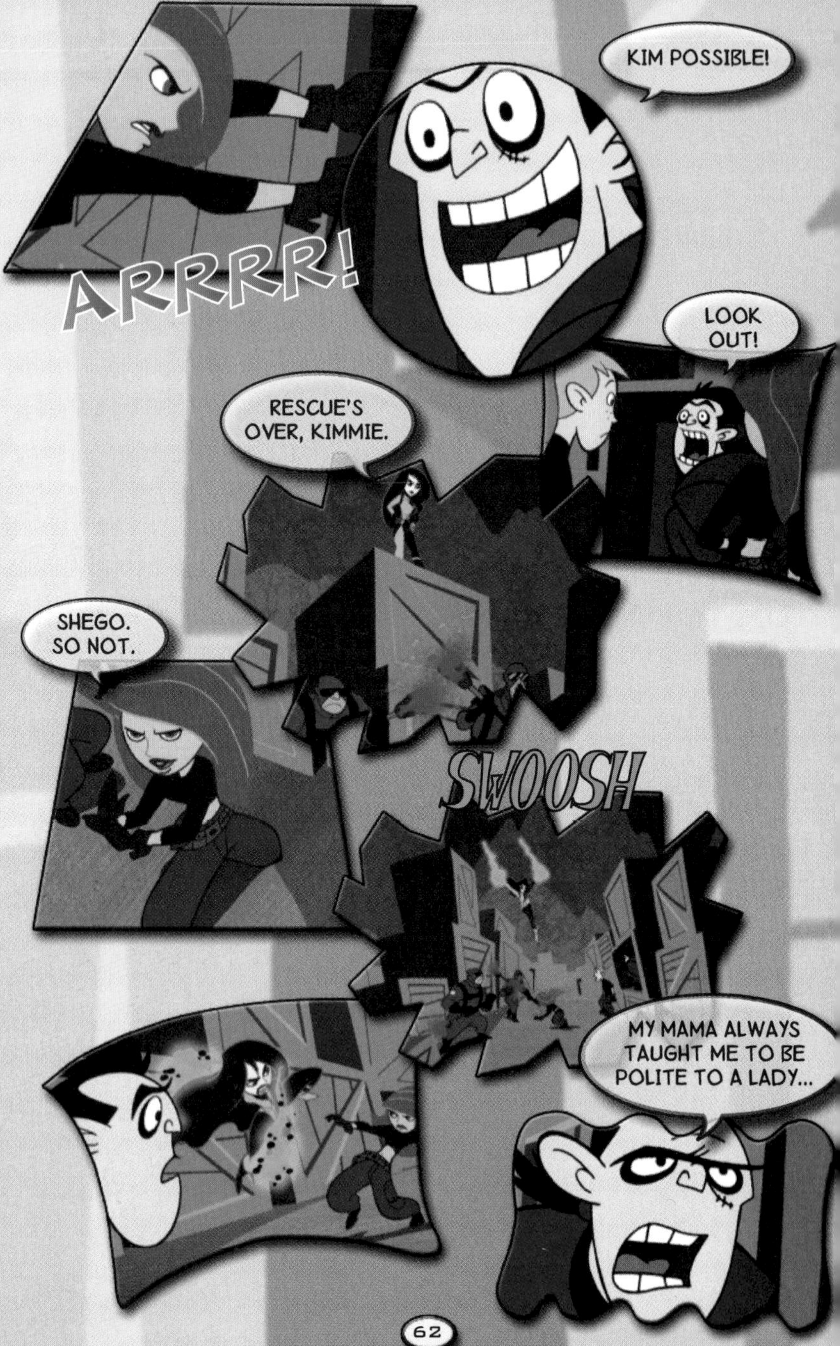
KIM POSSIBLE!
ARRRR!
LOOK OUT!
RESCUE'S OVER, KIMMIE.
SHEGO. SO NOT.
SWOOSH
MY MAMA ALWAYS TAUGHT ME TO BE POLITE TO A LADY...

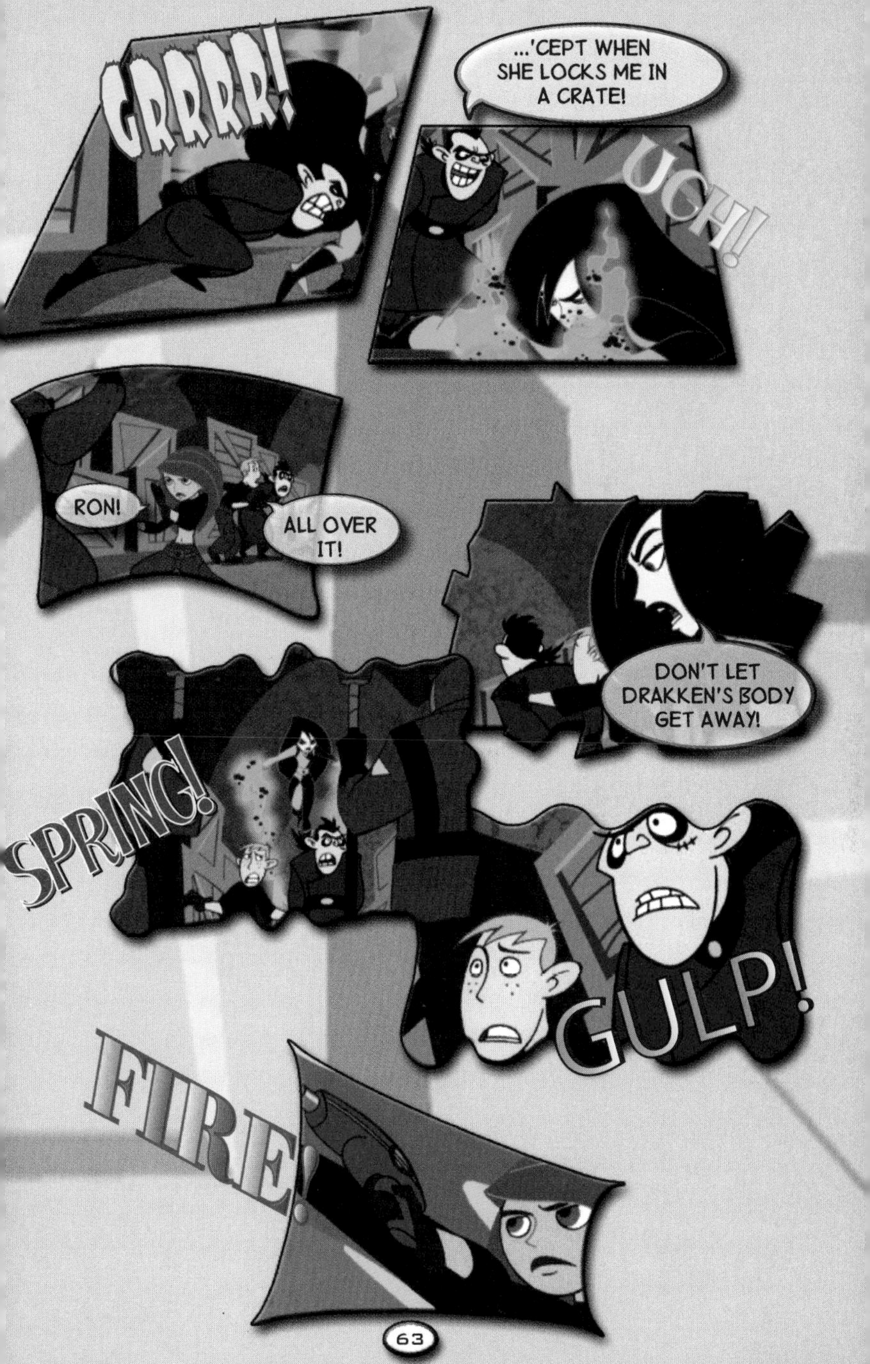
GRRRR!
...'CEPT WHEN SHE LOCKS ME IN A CRATE!
UGH!
RON!
ALL OVER IT!
DON'T LET DRAKKEN'S BODY GET AWAY!
SPRING!
GULP!
FIRE!

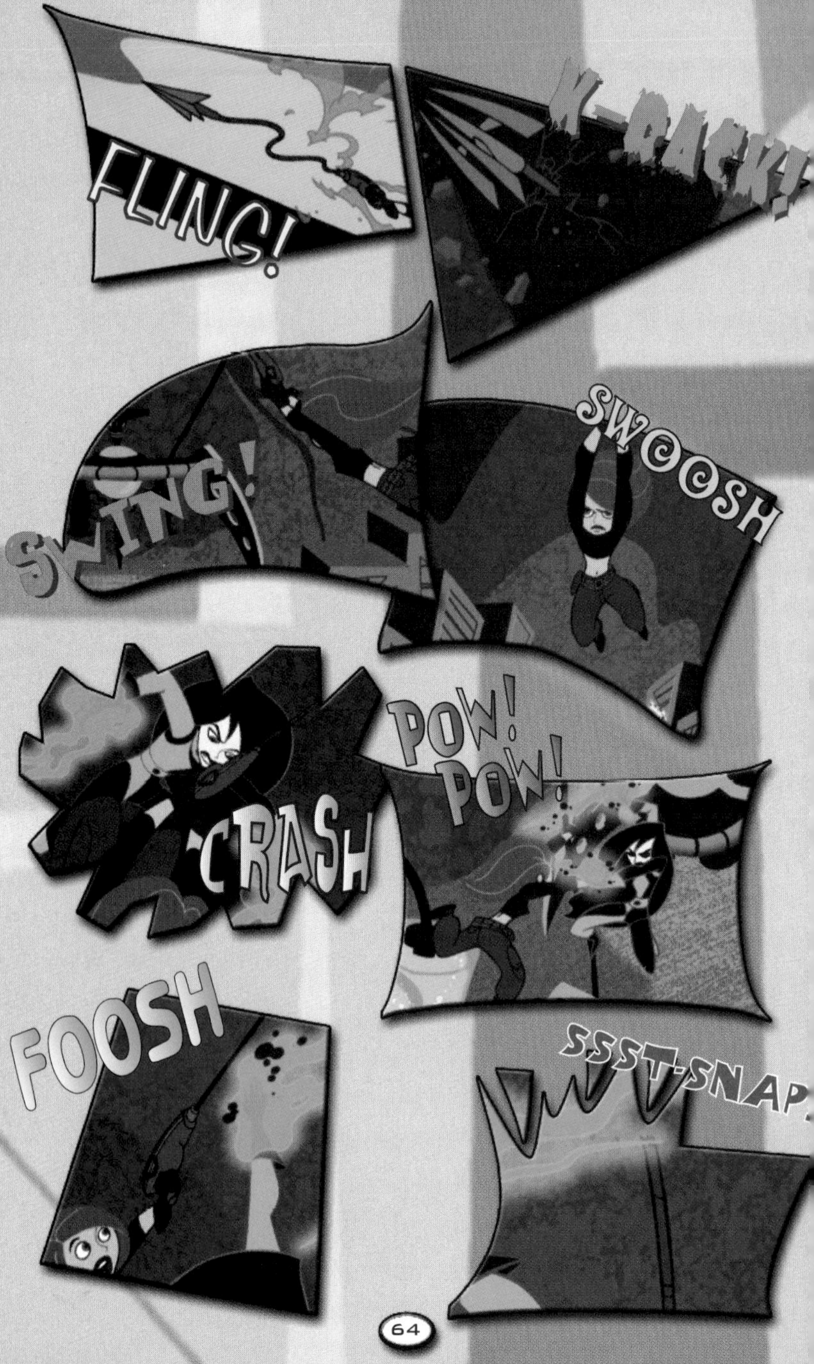
FLING!
K-RACK!
SWING!
SWOOSH
CRASH
POW! POW!
FOOSH
SSST-SNAP!

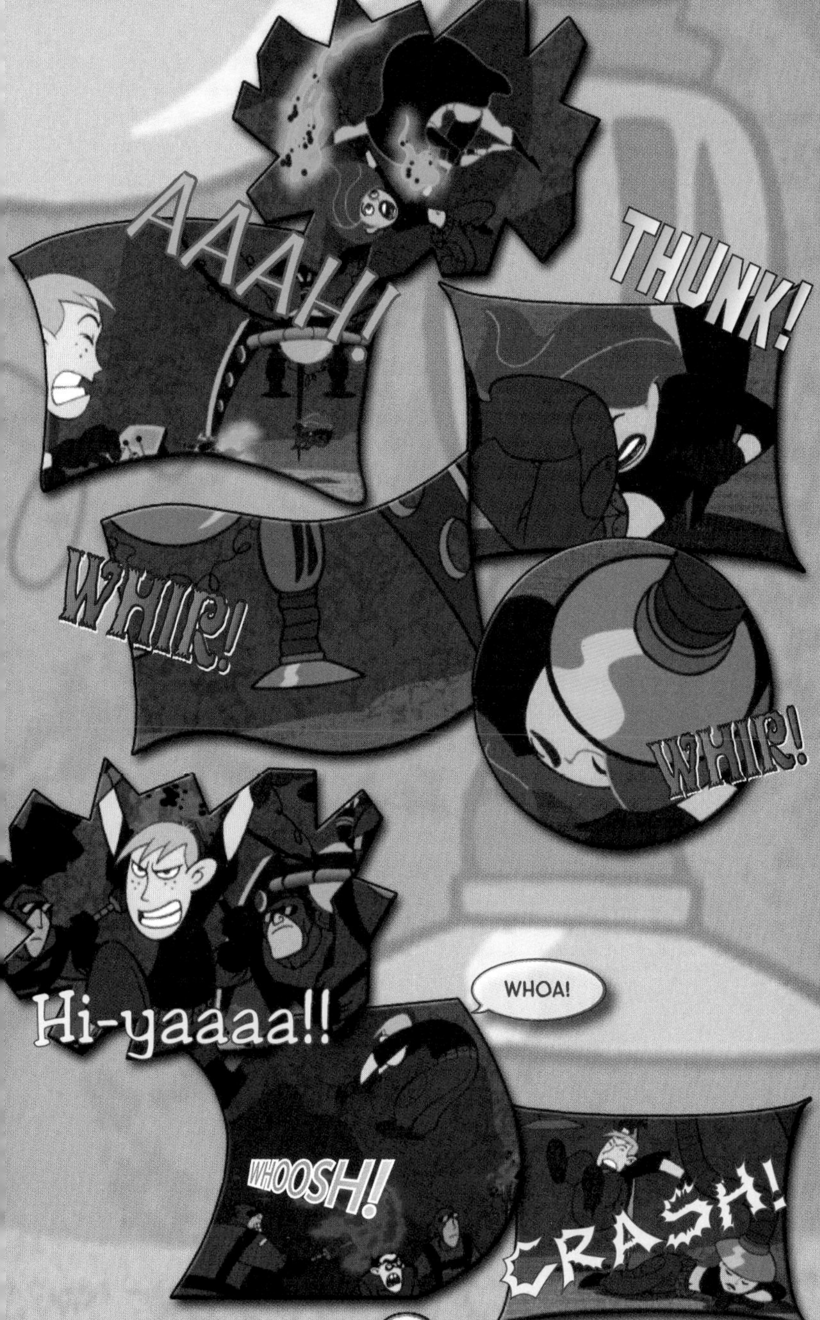
AAAH!
THUNK!
WHIR!
WHIR!
Hi-yaaaa!!
WHOA!
WHOOSH!
CRASH!

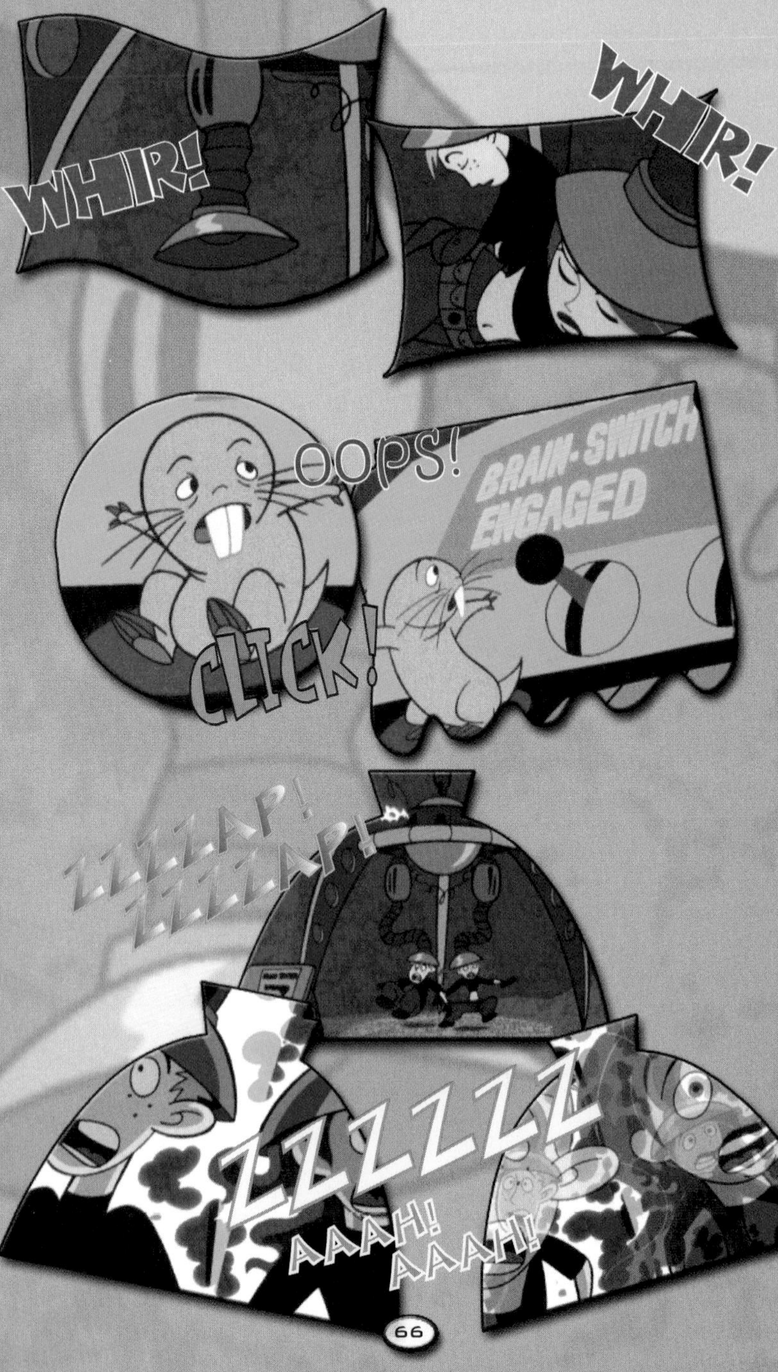
WHIR!
WHIR!
OOPS!
BRAIN-SWITCH
ENGAGED
CLICK!
ZZZZAP!
ZZZZAP!
ZZZZZZ
AAAH!
AAAH!

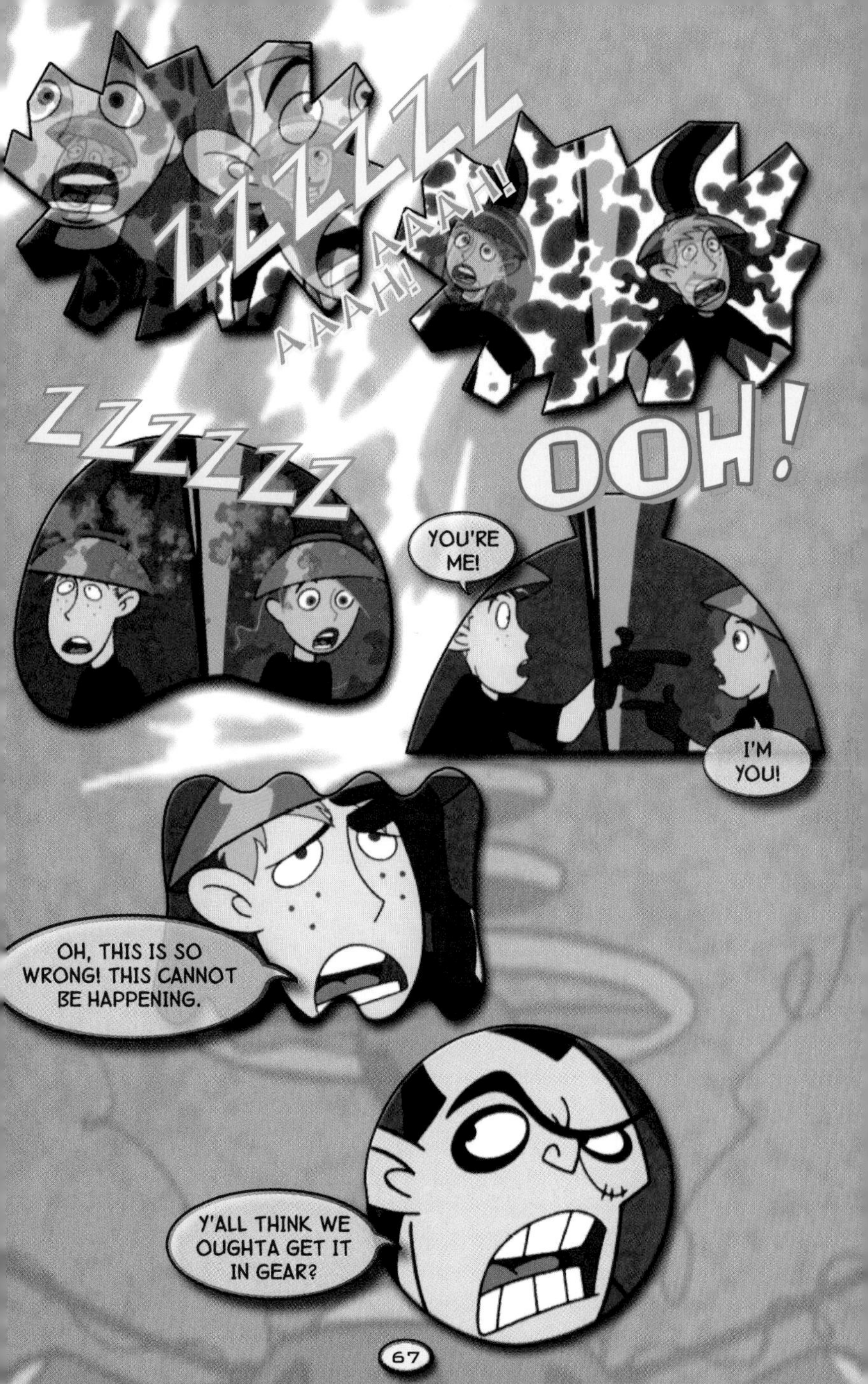
ZZZZZZZ
AAAH! AAAAH!
ZZZZZZZ
OOH!
YOU'RE ME!
I'M YOU!
OH, THIS IS SO WRONG! THIS CANNOT BE HAPPENING.
Y'ALL THINK WE OUGHTA GET IT IN GEAR?

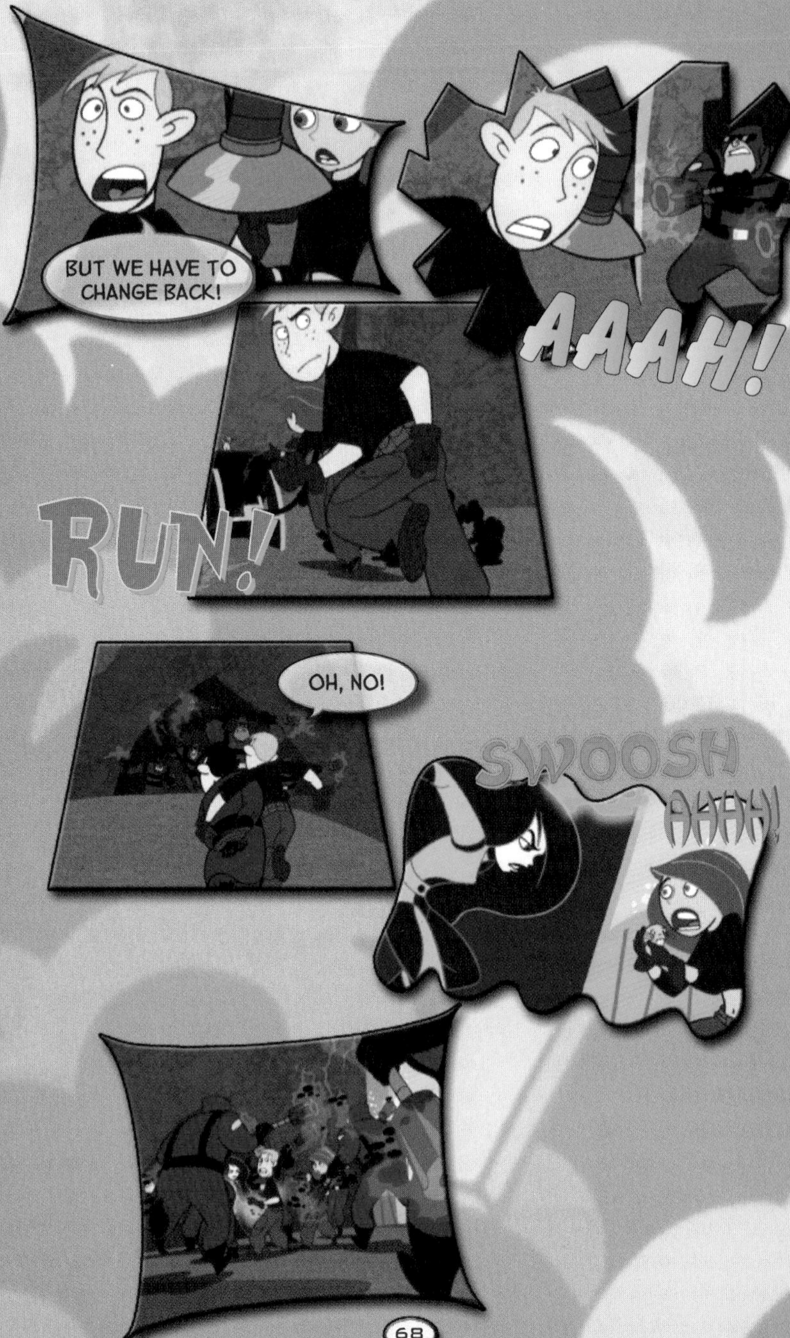
BUT WE HAVE TO CHANGE BACK!
AAAAH!
RUN!
OH, NO!
SWOOSH
AHHH!

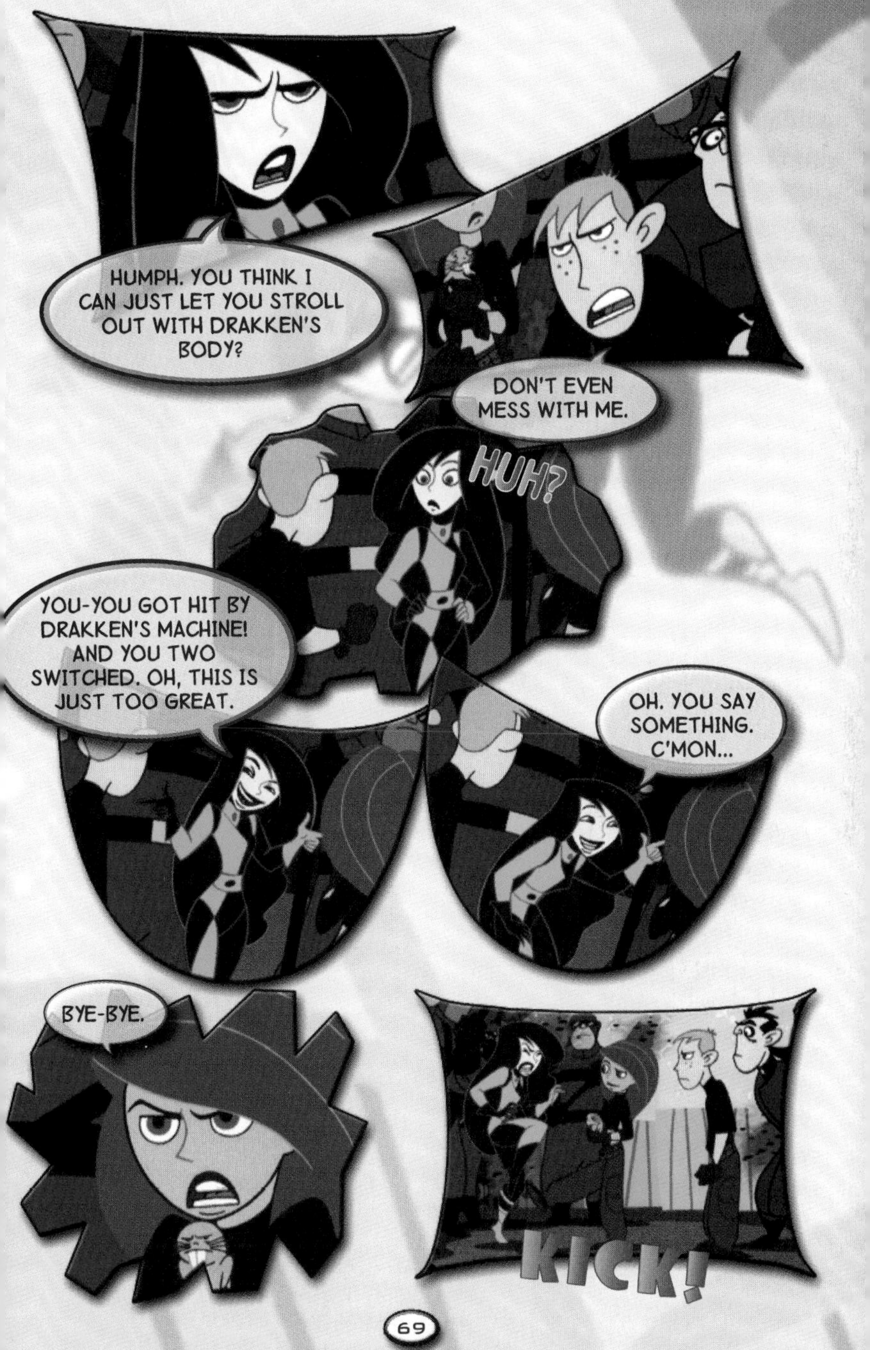
HUMPH. YOU THINK I CAN JUST LET YOU STROLL OUT WITH DRAKKEN'S BODY?
DON'T EVEN MESS WITH ME.
HUH?
YOU-YOU GOT HIT BY DRAKKEN'S MACHINE! AND YOU TWO SWITCHED. OH, THIS IS JUST TOO GREAT.
OH. YOU SAY SOMETHING. C'MON...
BYE-BYE.
KICK!

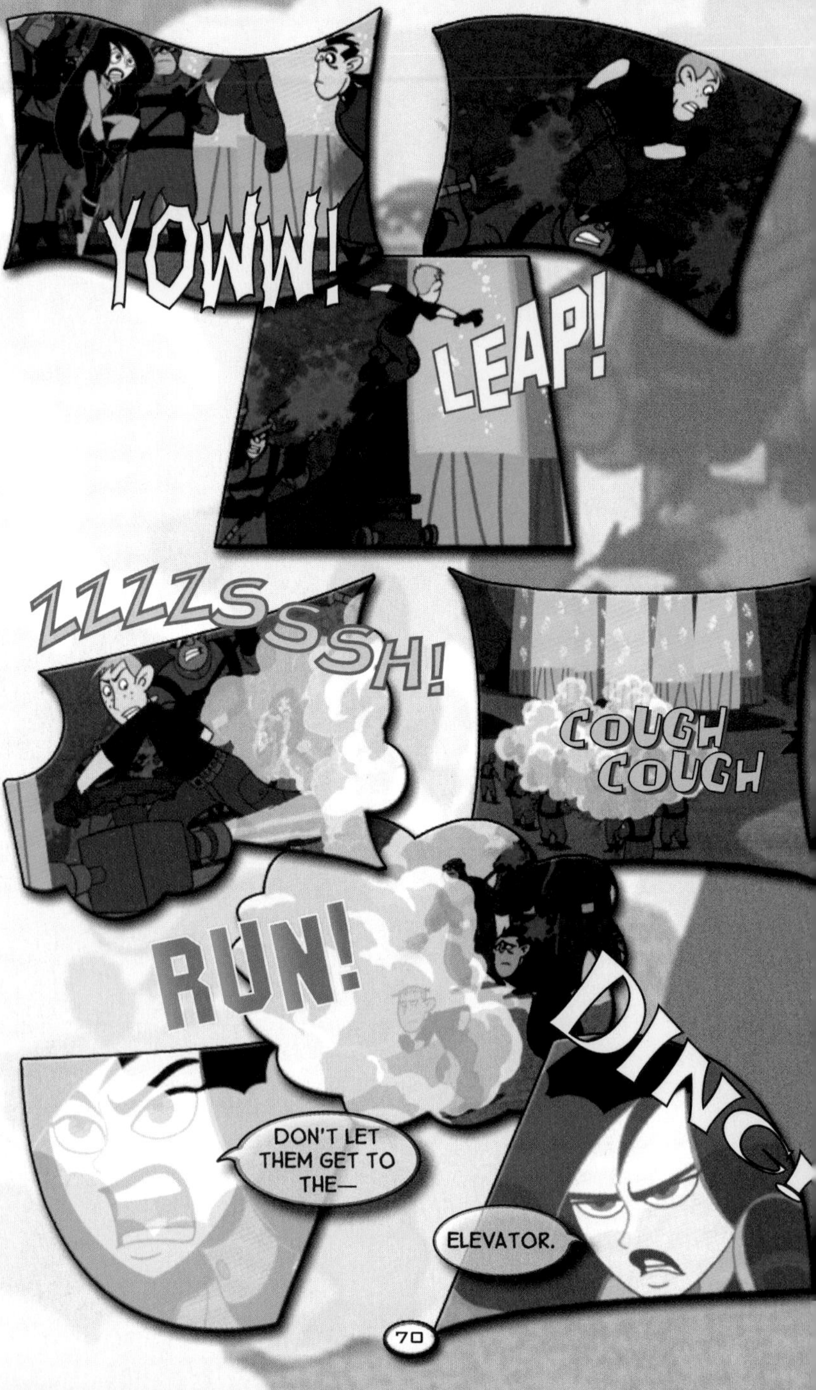
YOWW!
LEAP!
ZZZZSSSSH!
COUGH
COUGH
RUN!
DING!
DON'T LET THEM GET TO THE—
ELEVATOR.

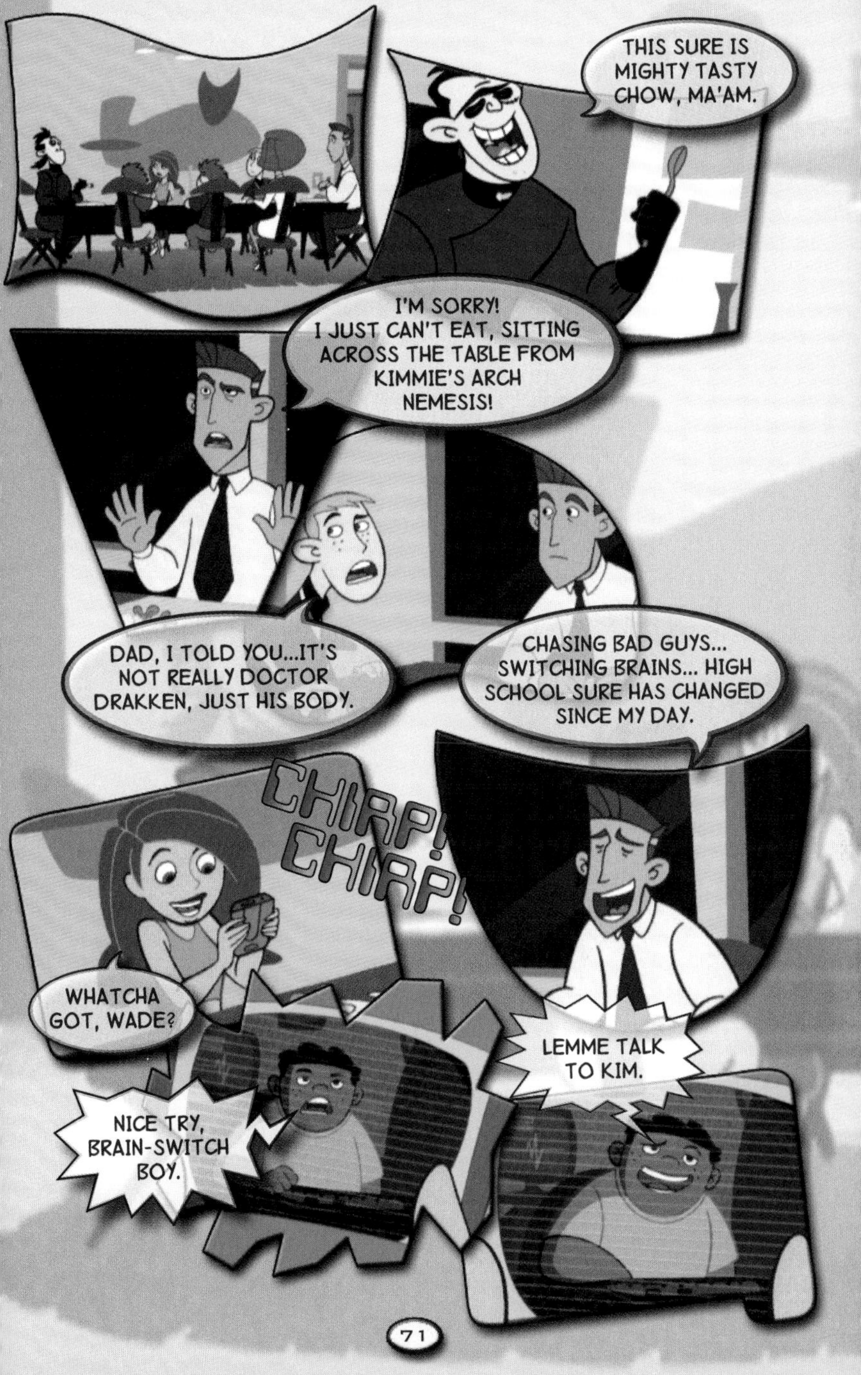
THIS SURE IS MIGHTY TASTY CHOW, MA'AM.
I'M SORRY! I JUST CAN'T EAT, SITTING ACROSS THE TABLE FROM KIMMIE'S ARCH NEMESIS!
DAD, I TOLD YOU...IT'S NOT REALLY DOCTOR DRAKKEN, JUST HIS BODY.
CHASING BAD GUYS... SWITCHING BRAINS... HIGH SCHOOL SURE HAS CHANGED SINCE MY DAY.
CHIRP! CHIRP!
WHATCHA GOT, WADE?
LEMME TALK TO KIM.
NICE TRY, BRAIN-SWITCH BOY.

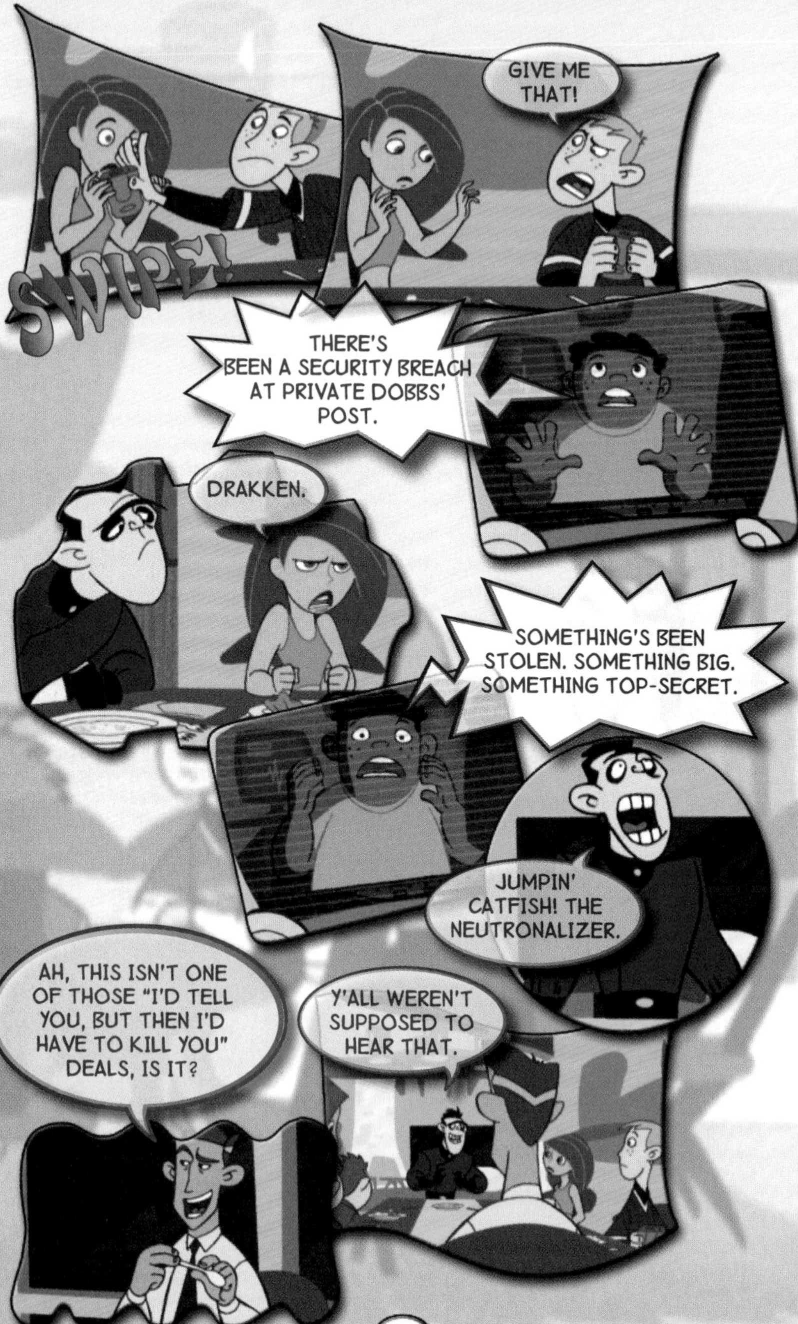
SWIPE!
GIVE ME THAT!
THERE'S BEEN A SECURITY BREACH AT PRIVATE DOBBS' POST.
DRAKKEN.
SOMETHING'S BEEN STOLEN. SOMETHING BIG. SOMETHING TOP-SECRET.
JUMPIN' CATFISH! THE NEUTRONALIZER.
AH, THIS ISN'T ONE OF THOSE "I'D TELL YOU, BUT THEN I'D HAVE TO KILL YOU" DEALS, IS IT?
Y'ALL WEREN'T SUPPOSED TO HEAR THAT.

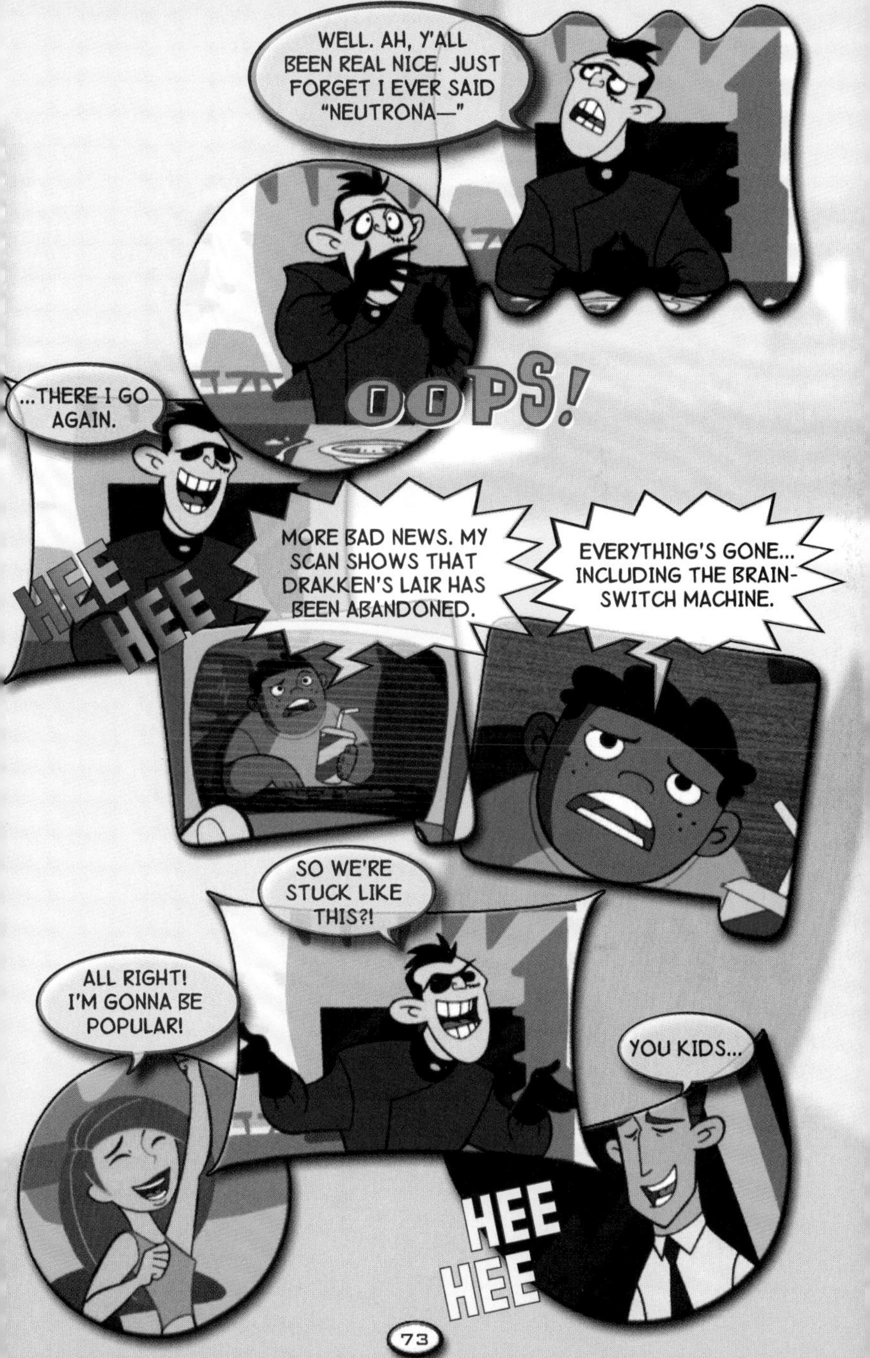

WELL. AH, Y'ALL BEEN REAL NICE. JUST FORGET I EVER SAID "NEUTRONA—"
OOPS!
...THERE I GO AGAIN.
HEE HEE
MORE BAD NEWS. MY SCAN SHOWS THAT DRAKKEN'S LAIR HAS BEEN ABANDONED.
EVERYTHING'S GONE... INCLUDING THE BRAIN-SWITCH MACHINE.
SO WE'RE STUCK LIKE THIS?!
ALL RIGHT! I'M GONNA BE POPULAR!
YOU KIDS...
HEE HEE

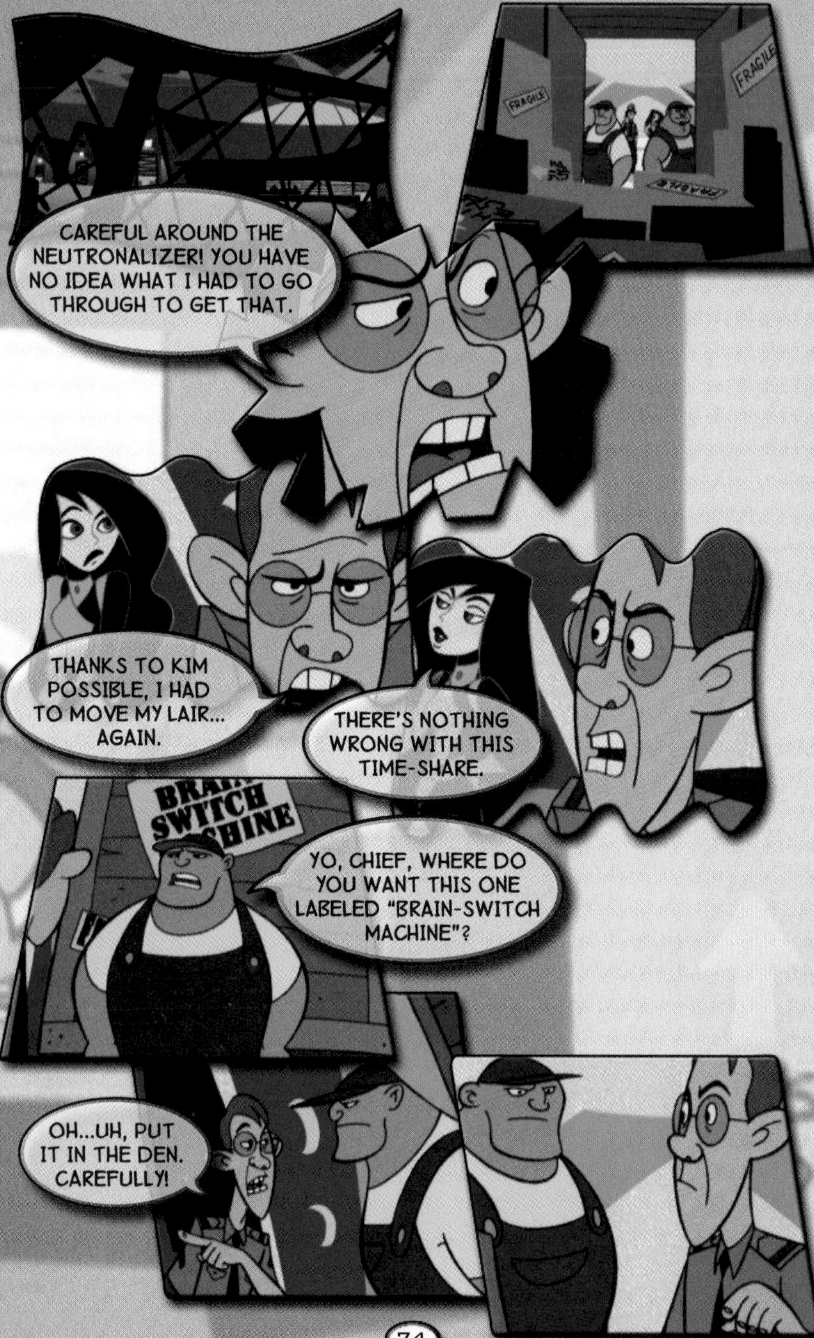
FRAGILE
CAREFUL AROUND THE NEUTRONALIZER! YOU HAVE NO IDEA WHAT I HAD TO GO THROUGH TO GET THAT.
THANKS TO KIM POSSIBLE, I HAD TO MOVE MY LAIR... AGAIN.
THERE'S NOTHING WRONG WITH THIS TIME-SHARE.
YO, CHIEF, WHERE DO YOU WANT THIS ONE LABELED "BRAIN-SWITCH MACHINE"?
OH...UH, PUT IT IN THE DEN. CAREFULLY!

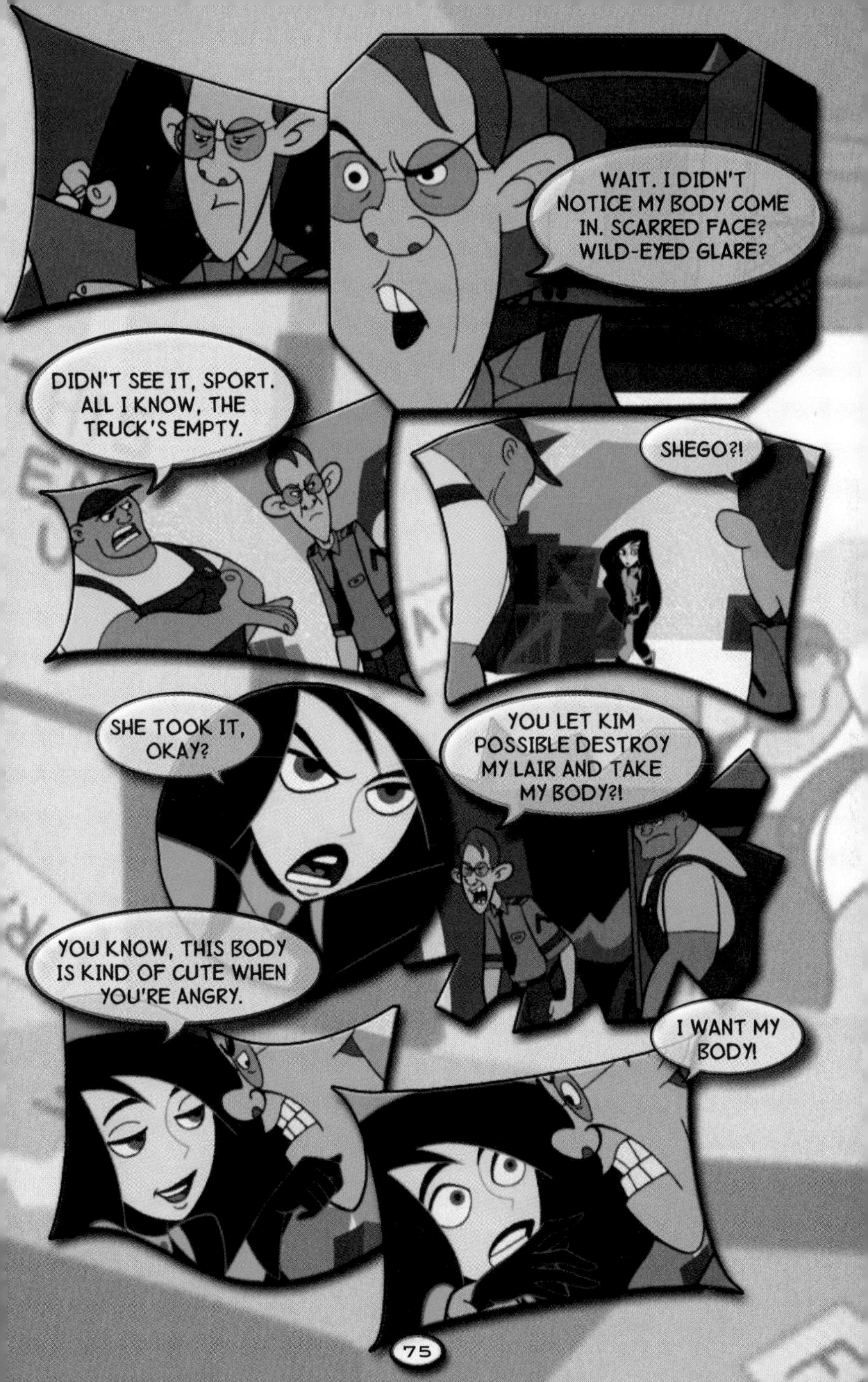
WAIT. I DIDN'T NOTICE MY BODY COME IN. SCARRED FACE? WILD-EYED GLARE?
DIDN'T SEE IT, SPORT. ALL I KNOW, THE TRUCK'S EMPTY.
SHEGO?!
SHE TOOK IT, OKAY?
YOU LET KIM POSSIBLE DESTROY MY LAIR AND TAKE MY BODY?!
YOU KNOW, THIS BODY IS KIND OF CUTE WHEN YOU'RE ANGRY.
I WANT MY BODY!

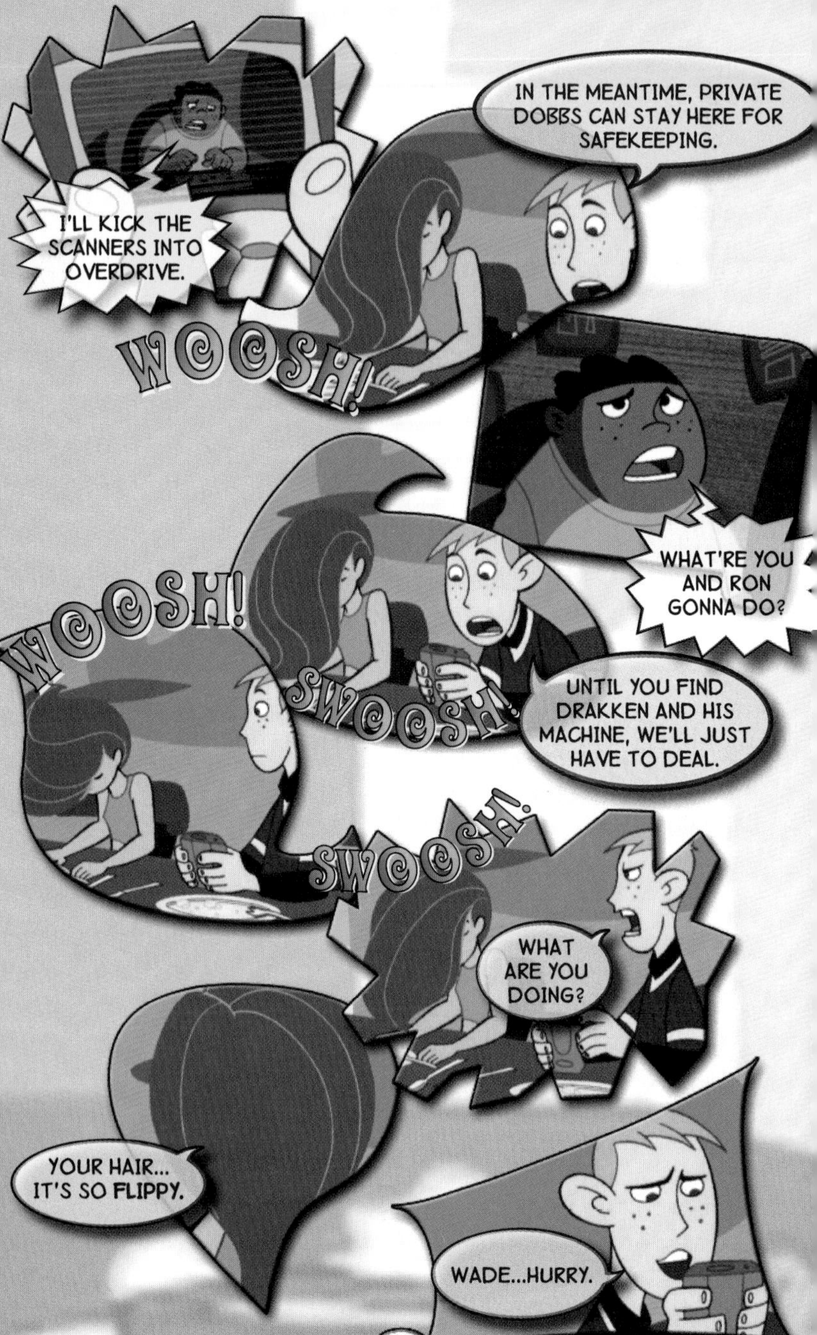
IN THE MEANTIME, PRIVATE DOBBS CAN STAY HERE FOR SAFEKEEPING.
I'LL KICK THE SCANNERS INTO OVERDRIVE.
WOOSH!
WHAT'RE YOU AND RON GONNA DO?
WOOSH!
SWOOSH!
UNTIL YOU FIND DRAKKEN AND HIS MACHINE, WE'LL JUST HAVE TO DEAL.
SWOOSH!
WHAT ARE YOU DOING?
YOUR HAIR... IT'S SO FLIPPY.
WADE...HURRY.

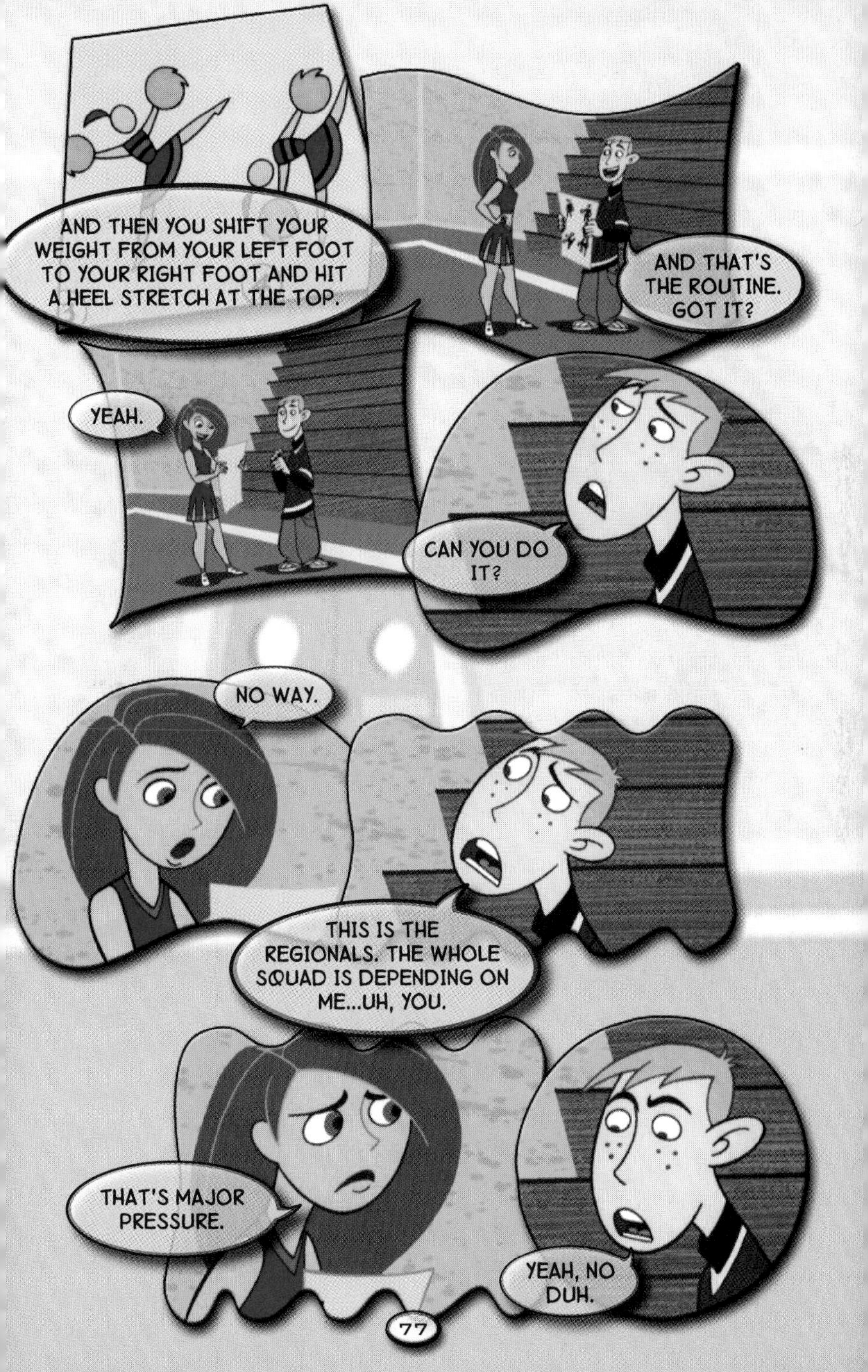
AND THEN YOU SHIFT YOUR WEIGHT FROM YOUR LEFT FOOT TO YOUR RIGHT FOOT AND HIT A HEEL STRETCH AT THE TOP.
AND THAT'S THE ROUTINE. GOT IT?
YEAH.
CAN YOU DO IT?
NO WAY.
THIS IS THE REGIONALS. THE WHOLE SQUAD IS DEPENDING ON ME...UH, YOU.
THAT'S MAJOR PRESSURE.
YEAH, NO DUH.

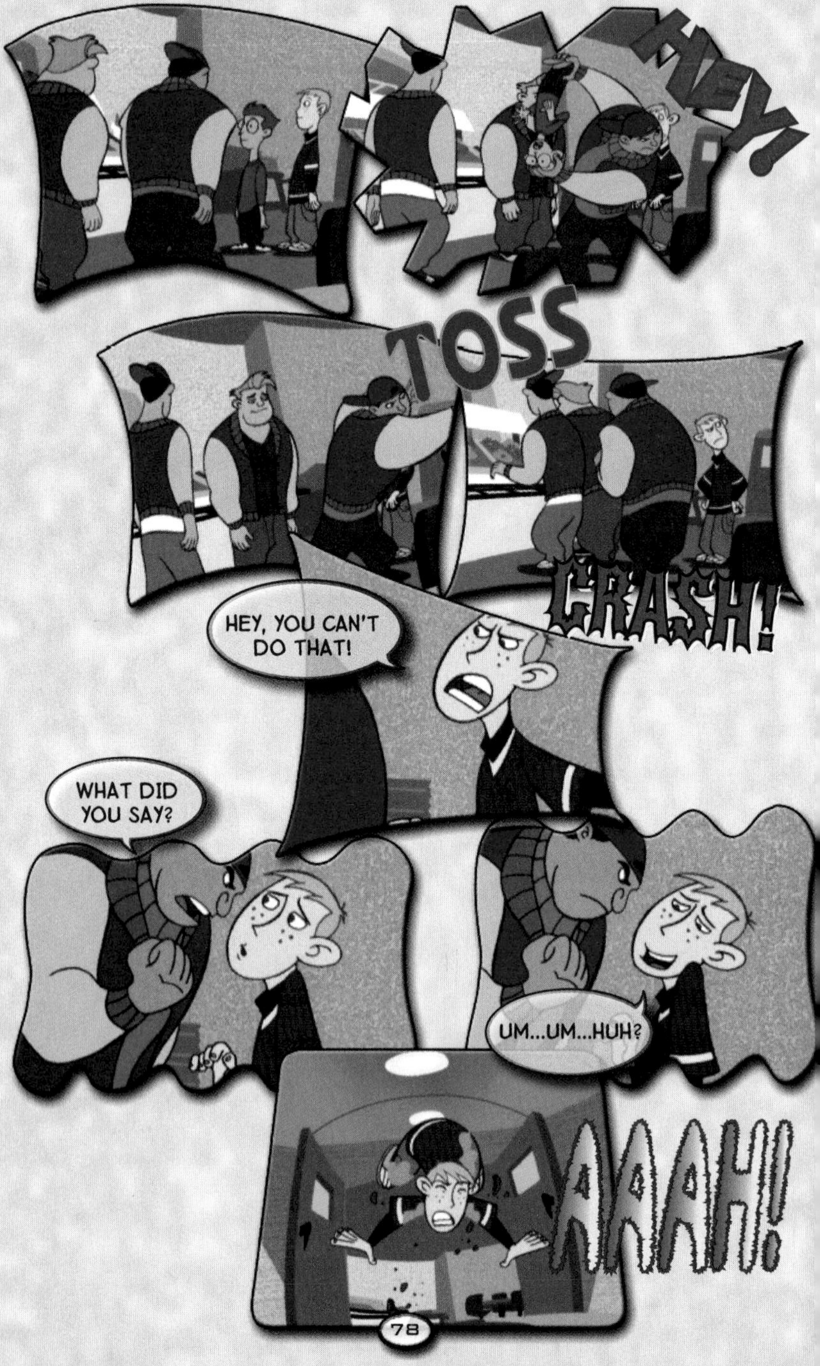
HEY!
TOSS
CRASH!
HEY, YOU CAN'T DO THAT!
WHAT DID YOU SAY?
UM...UM...HUH?
AAAH!

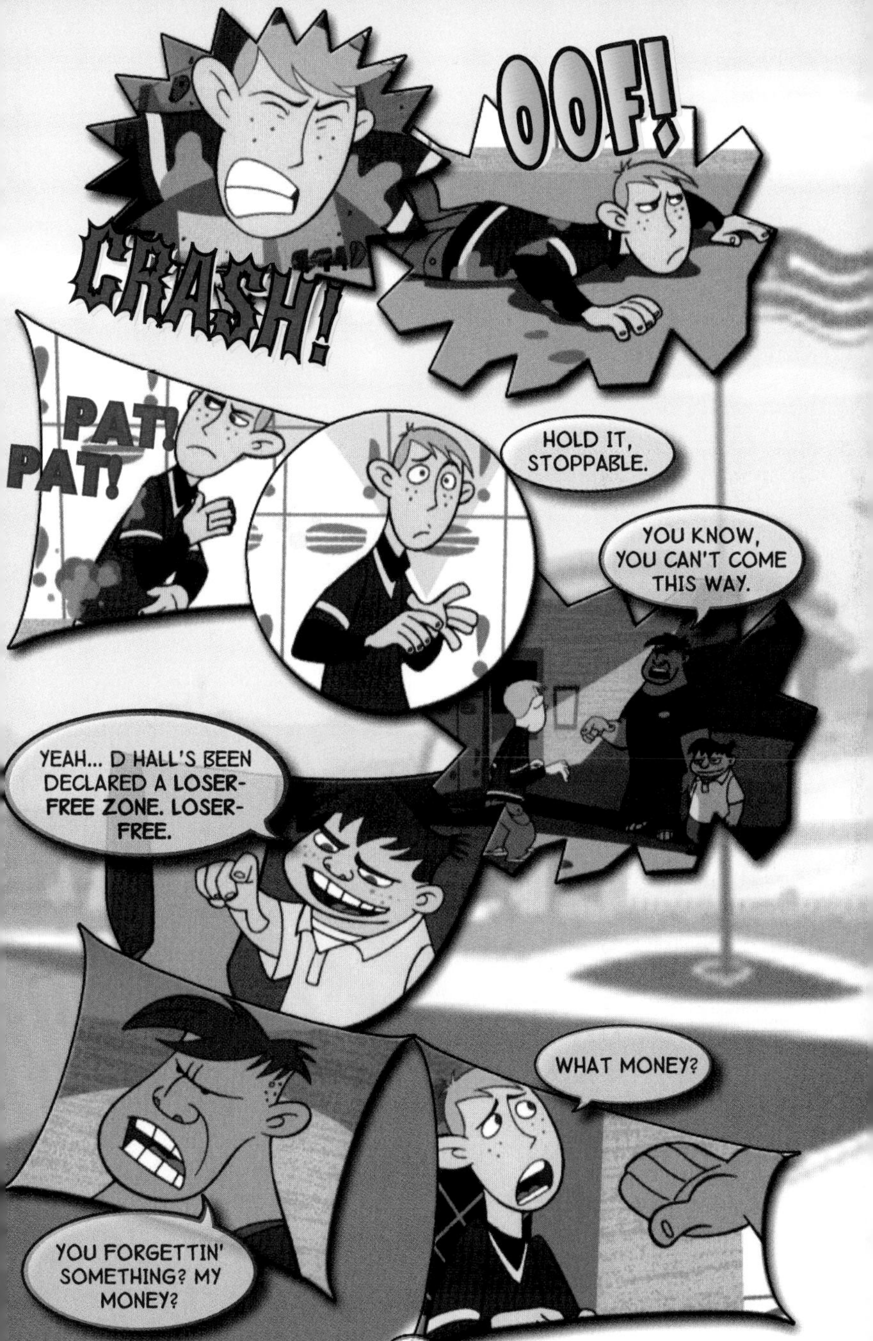
CRASH!
OOF!
PAT!
PAT!
HOLD IT, STOPPABLE.
YOU KNOW, YOU CAN'T COME THIS WAY.
YEAH... D HALL'S BEEN DECLARED A LOSER-FREE ZONE. LOSER-FREE.
YOU FORGETTIN' SOMETHING? MY MONEY?
WHAT MONEY?

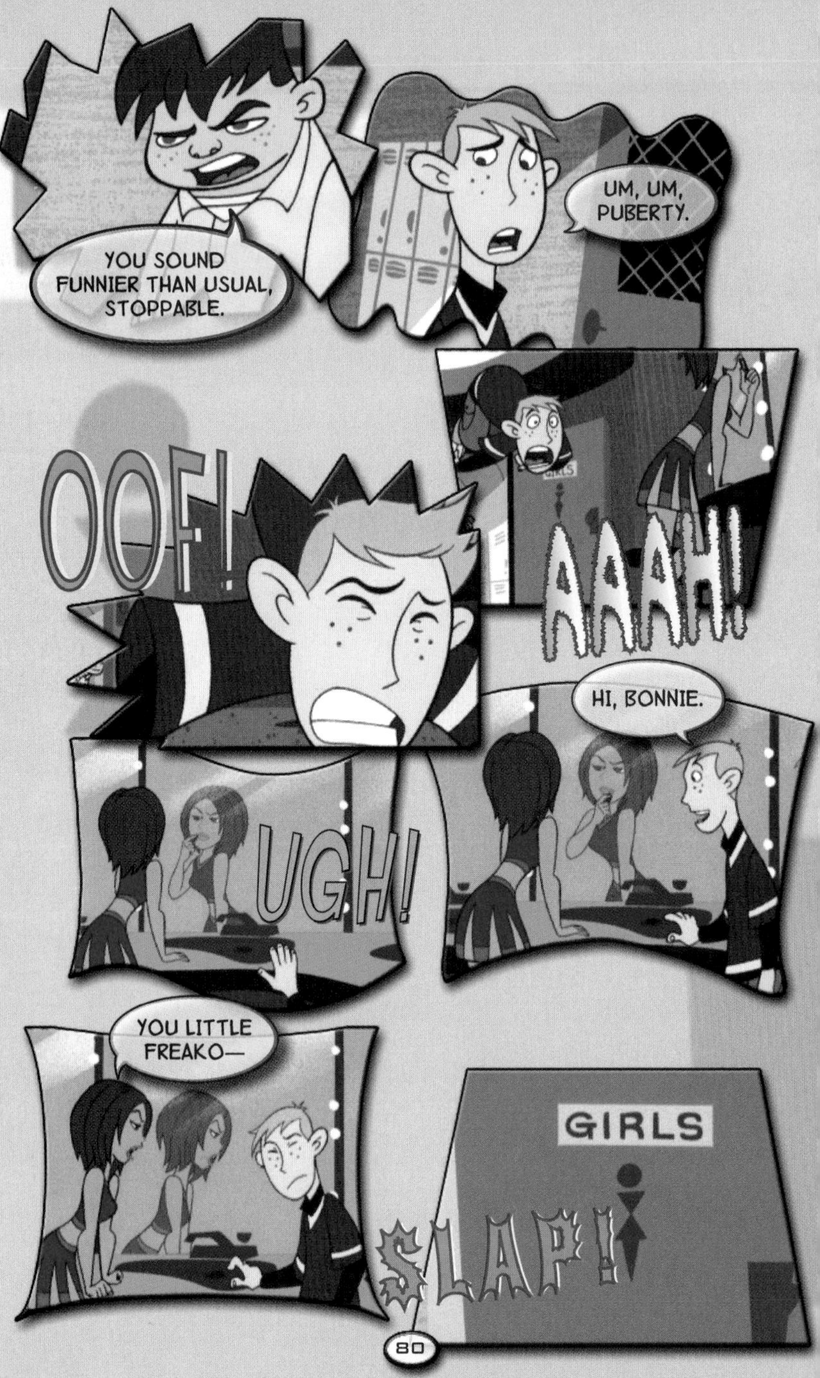

YOU SOUND FUNNIER THAN USUAL, STOPPABLE.
UM, UM, PUBERTY.
OOF!
AAAH!
HI, BONNIE.
UGH!
YOU LITTLE FREAKO—
GIRLS
SLAP!

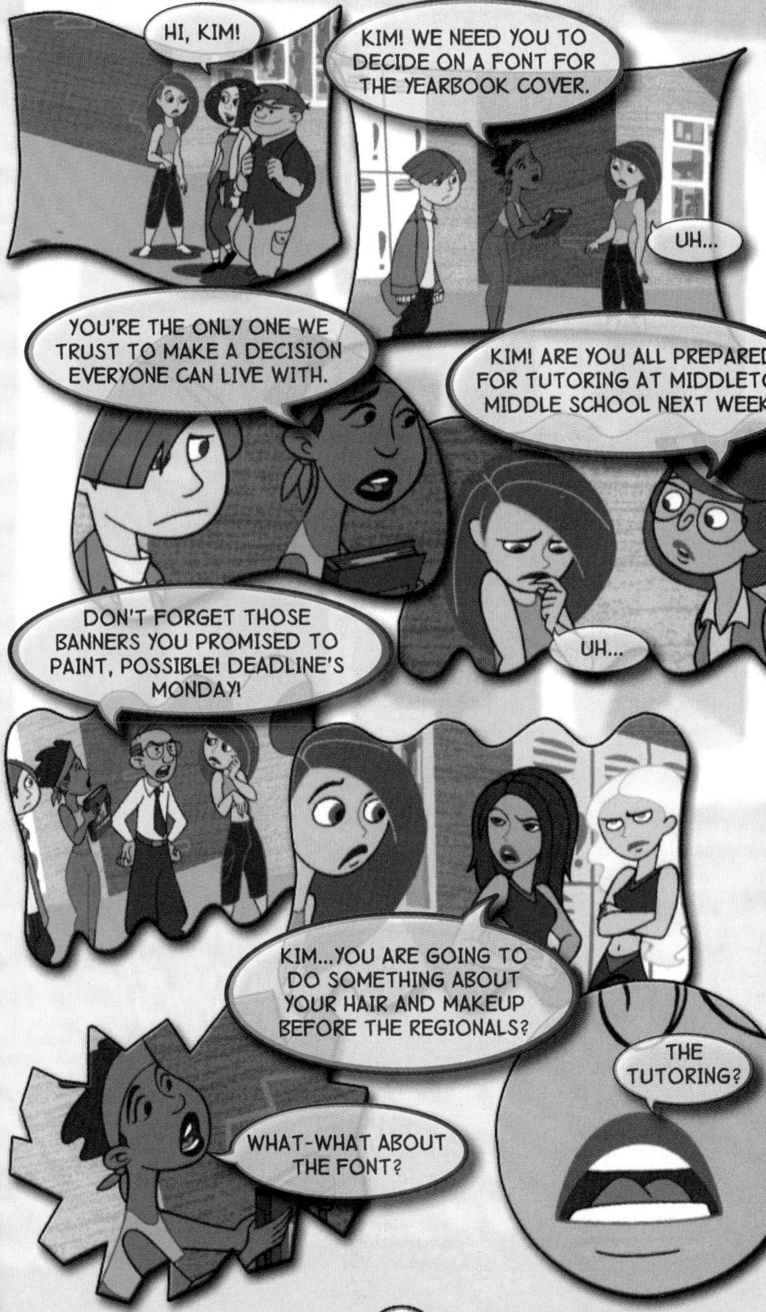
HI, KIM!
KIM! WE NEED YOU TO DECIDE ON A FONT FOR THE YEARBOOK COVER.
UH...
YOU'RE THE ONLY ONE WE TRUST TO MAKE A DECISION EVERYONE CAN LIVE WITH.
KIM! ARE YOU ALL PREPARED FOR TUTORING AT MIDDLETON MIDDLE SCHOOL NEXT WEEK?
UH...
DON'T FORGET THOSE BANNERS YOU PROMISED TO PAINT, POSSIBLE! DEADLINE'S MONDAY!
KIM...YOU ARE GOING TO DO SOMETHING ABOUT YOUR HAIR AND MAKEUP BEFORE THE REGIONALS?
THE TUTORING?
WHAT-WHAT ABOUT THE FONT?

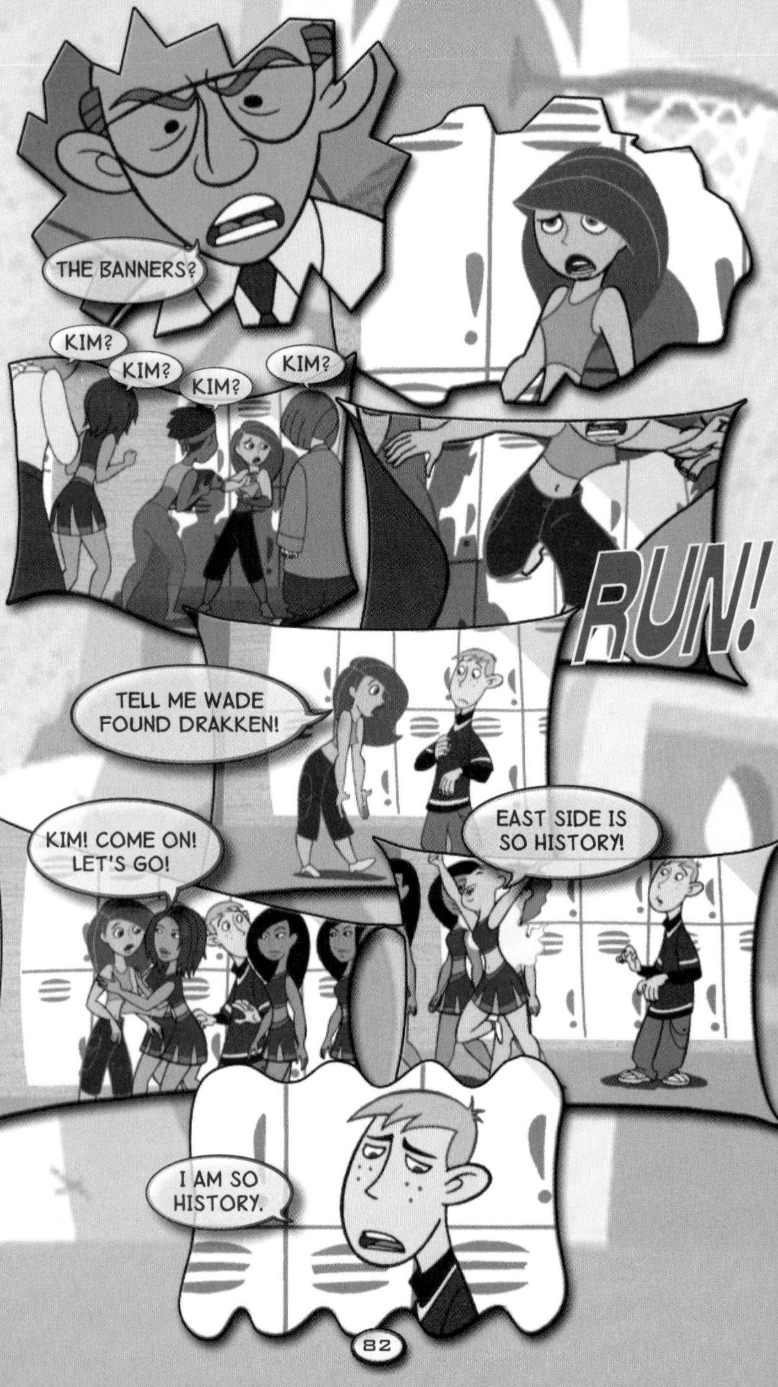
THE BANNERS?
KIM?
KIM?
KIM?
KIM?
RUN!
TELL ME WADE
FOUND DRAKKEN!
KIM! COME ON!
LET'S GO!
EAST SIDE IS
SO HISTORY!
I AM SO
HISTORY.

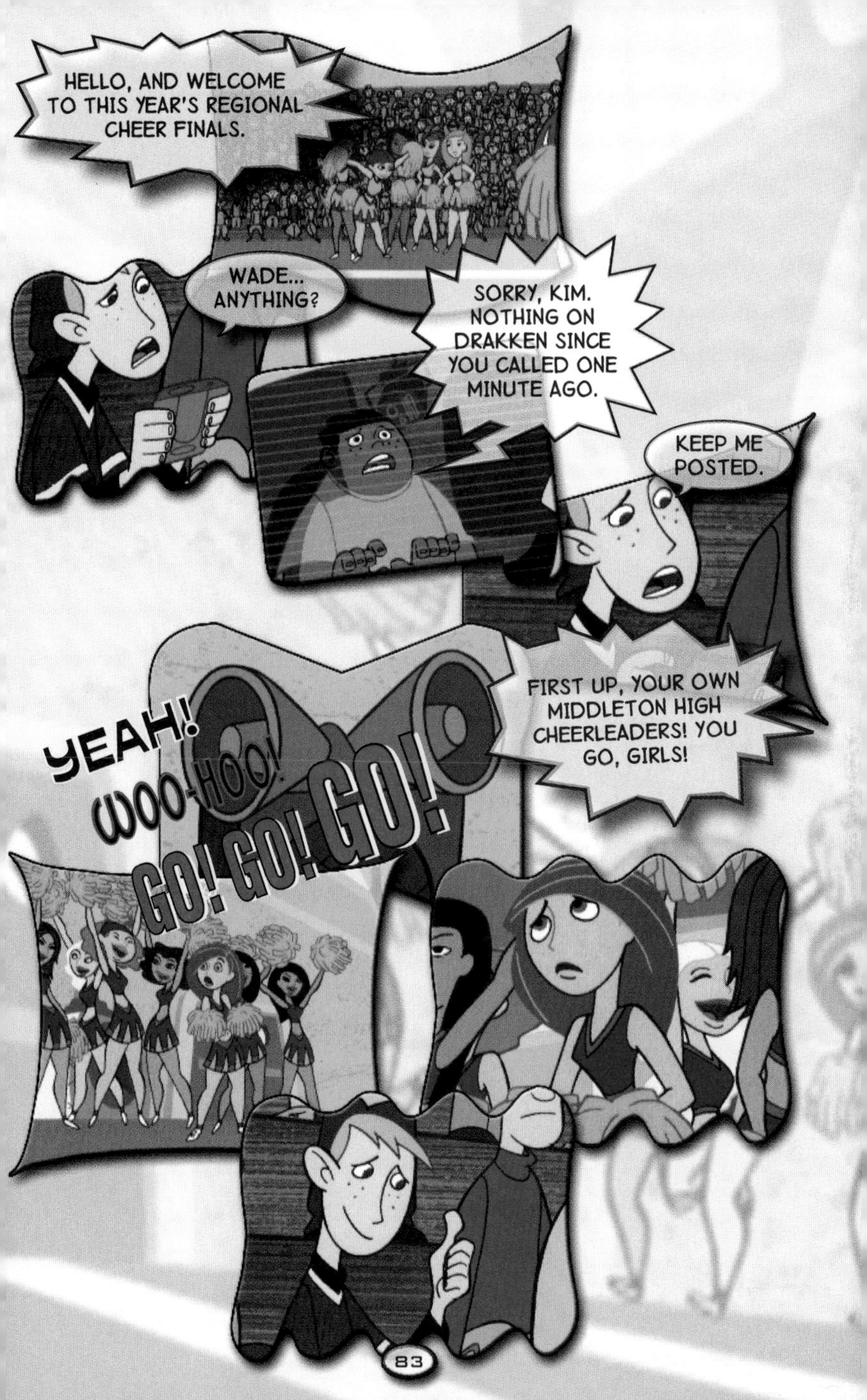
HELLO, AND WELCOME TO THIS YEAR'S REGIONAL CHEER FINALS.
WADE... ANYTHING?
SORRY, KIM. NOTHING ON DRAKKEN SINCE YOU CALLED ONE MINUTE AGO.
KEEP ME POSTED.
FIRST UP, YOUR OWN MIDDLETON HIGH CHEERLEADERS! YOU GO, GIRLS!
YEAH!
WOO-HOO!
GO! GO! GO!

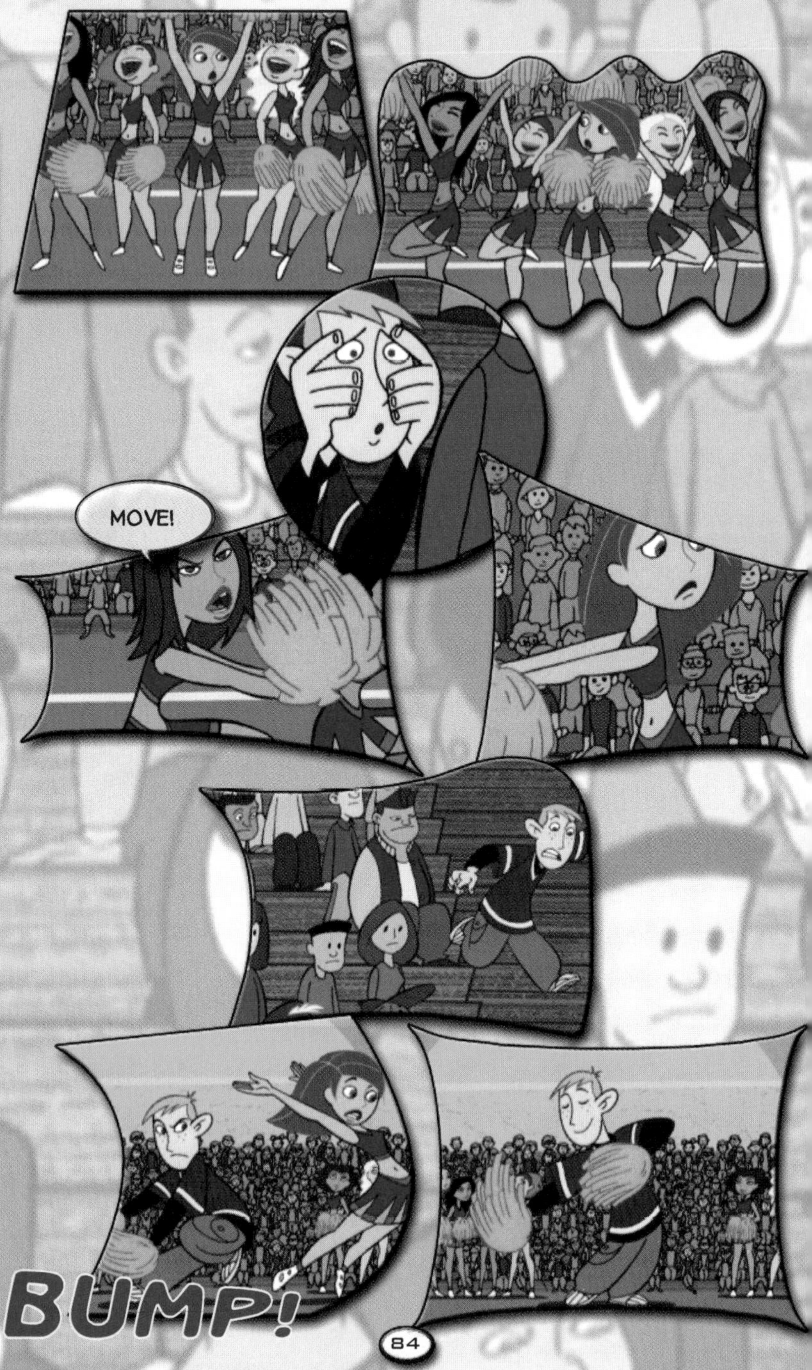
MOVE!
BUMP!

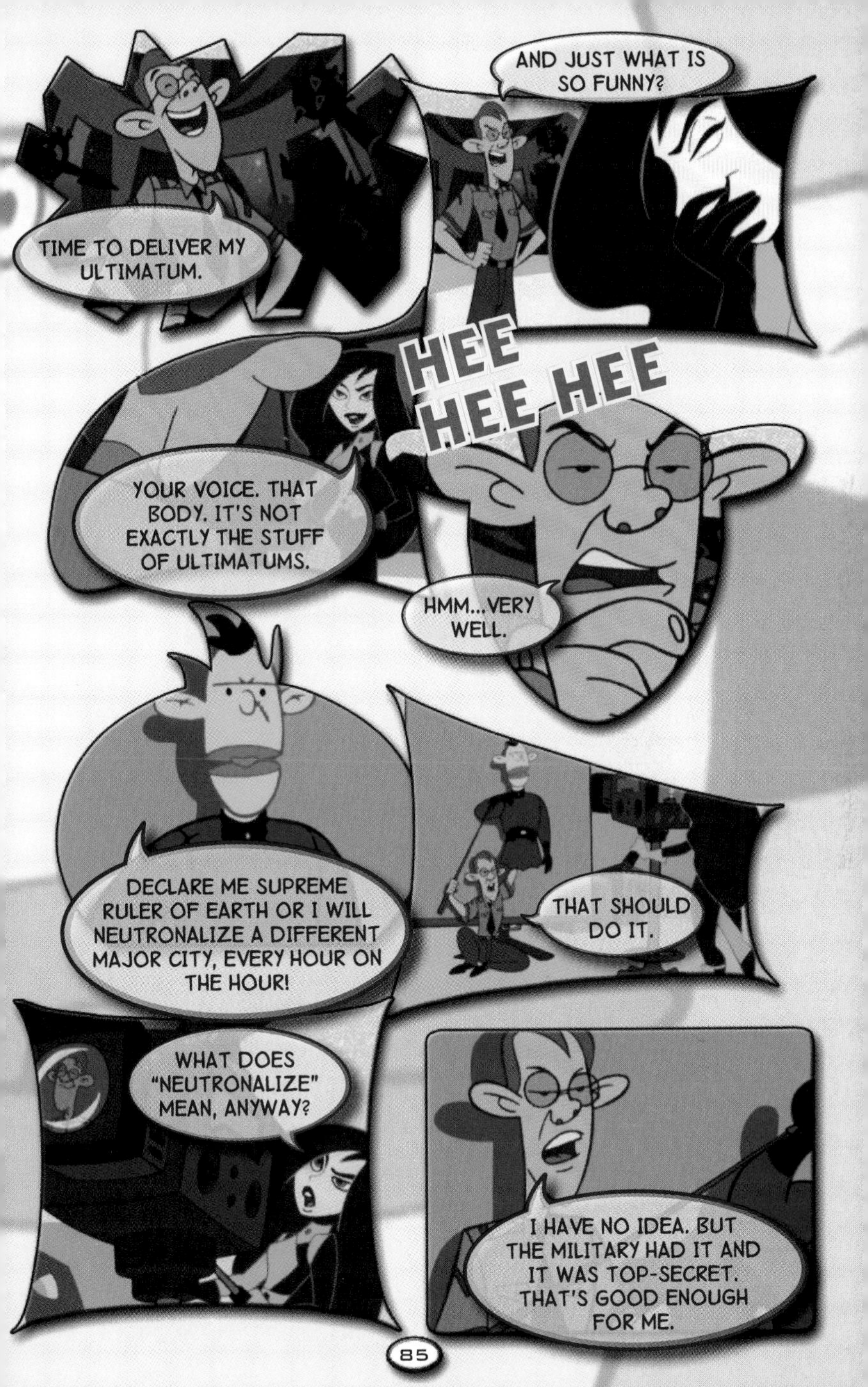
TIME TO DELIVER MY ULTIMATUM.
AND JUST WHAT IS SO FUNNY?
HEE HEE HEE
YOUR VOICE. THAT BODY. IT'S NOT EXACTLY THE STUFF OF ULTIMATUMS.
HMM...VERY WELL.
DECLARE ME SUPREME RULER OF EARTH OR I WILL NEUTRONALIZE A DIFFERENT MAJOR CITY, EVERY HOUR ON THE HOUR!
THAT SHOULD DO IT.
WHAT DOES "NEUTRONALIZE" MEAN, ANYWAY?
I HAVE NO IDEA. BUT THE MILITARY HAD IT AND IT WAS TOP-SECRET. THAT'S GOOD ENOUGH FOR ME.

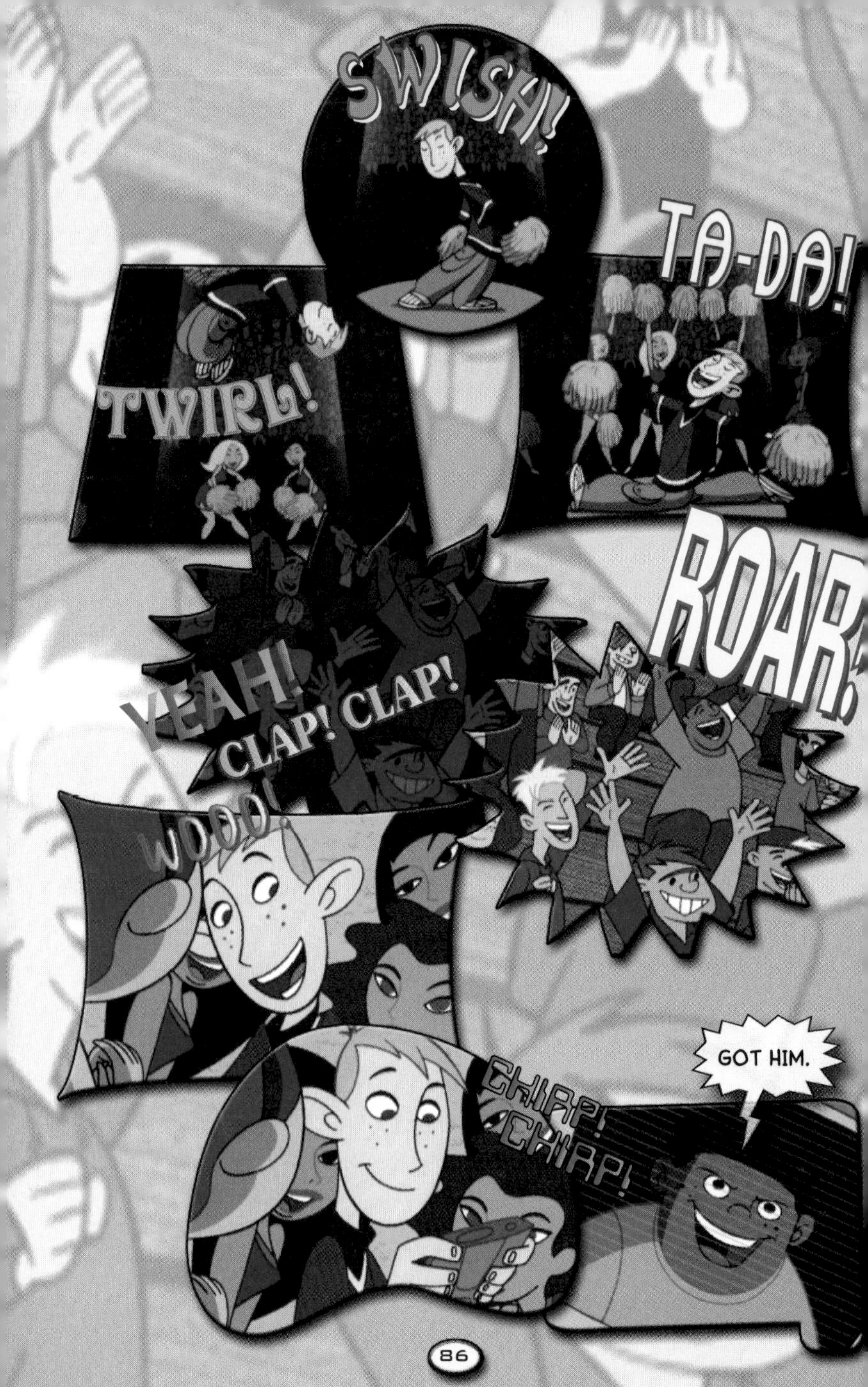
SWISH!
TA-DA!
TWIRL!
ROAR!
YEAH!
CLAP! CLAP!
WOOO!
CHIRP! CHIRP!
GOT HIM.

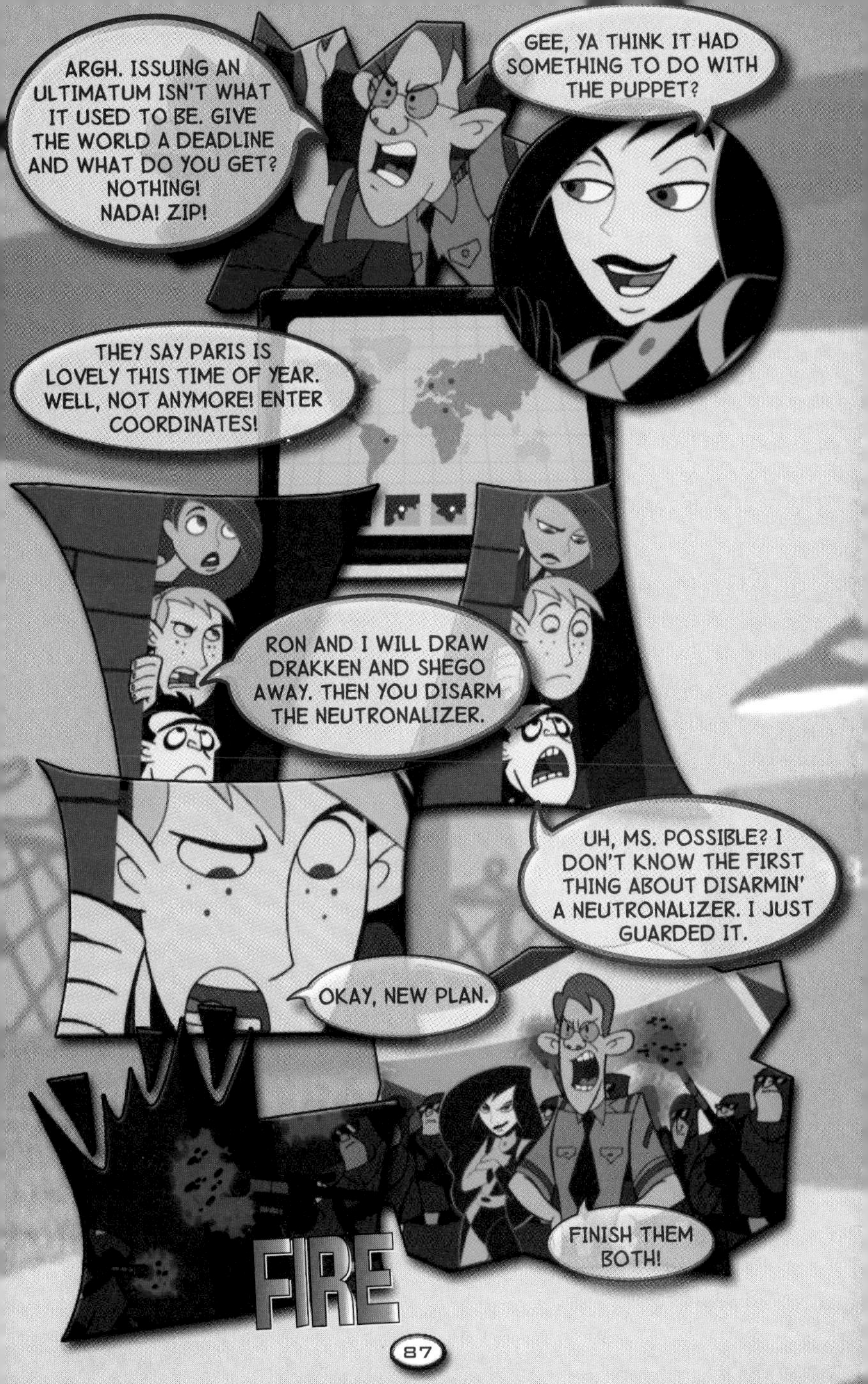
ARGH. ISSUING AN ULTIMATUM ISN'T WHAT IT USED TO BE. GIVE THE WORLD A DEADLINE AND WHAT DO YOU GET? NOTHING! NADA! ZIP!
GEE, YA THINK IT HAD SOMETHING TO DO WITH THE PUPPET?
THEY SAY PARIS IS LOVELY THIS TIME OF YEAR. WELL, NOT ANYMORE! ENTER COORDINATES!
RON AND I WILL DRAW DRAKKEN AND SHEGO AWAY. THEN YOU DISARM THE NEUTRONALIZER.
UH, MS. POSSIBLE? I DON'T KNOW THE FIRST THING ABOUT DISARMIN' A NEUTRONALIZER. I JUST GUARDED IT.
OKAY, NEW PLAN.
FINISH THEM BOTH!
FIRE

RUN!
KA-BLAMMO!
SHOOM!
WHOA!
BOOM!
BOOM!
BOOM!
I GOT HIM...HER...
I...WHATEVER. I GOT 'EM.

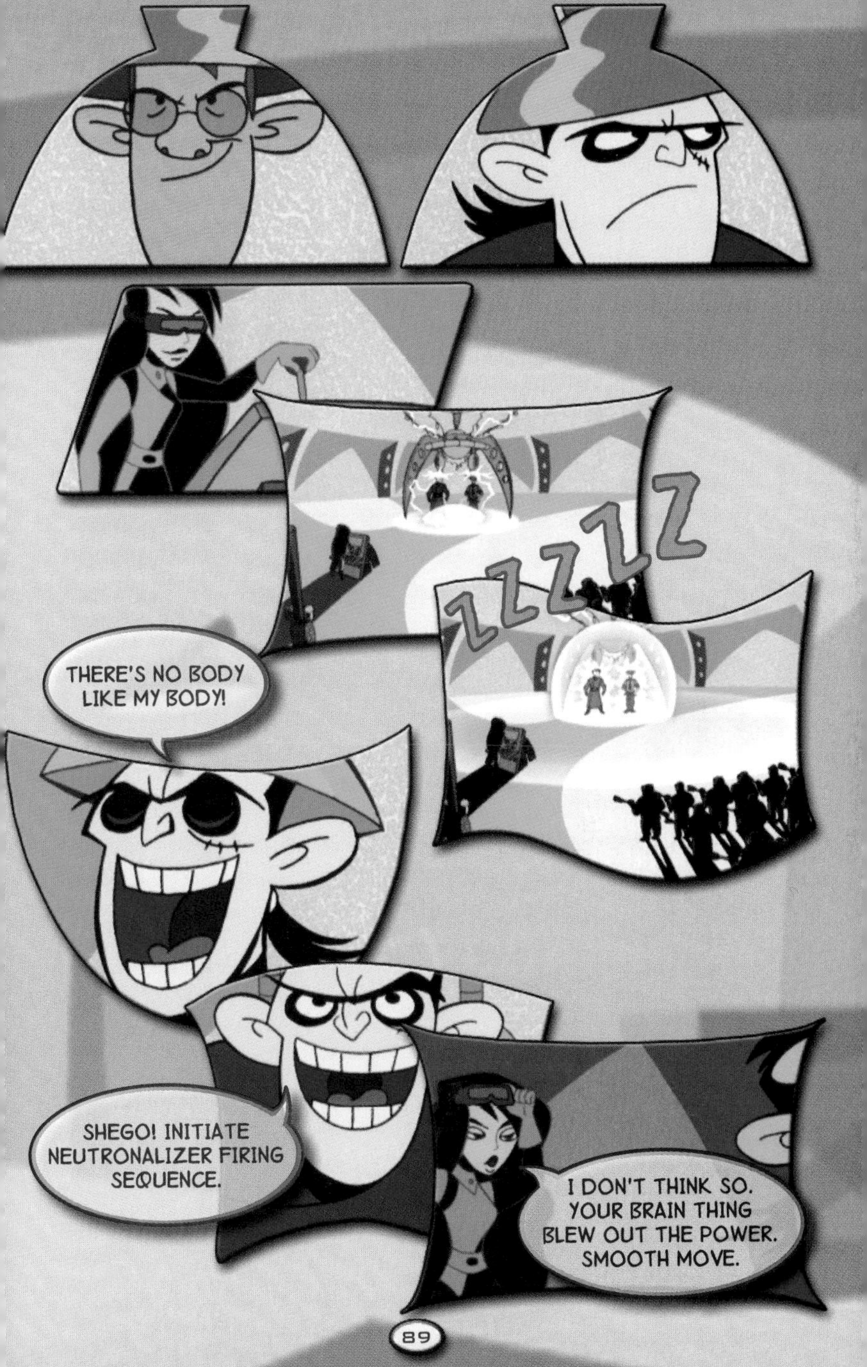
ZZZZZ
THERE'S NO BODY LIKE MY BODY!
SHEGO! INITIATE NEUTRONALIZER FIRING SEQUENCE.
I DON'T THINK SO. YOUR BRAIN THING BLEW OUT THE POWER. SMOOTH MOVE.

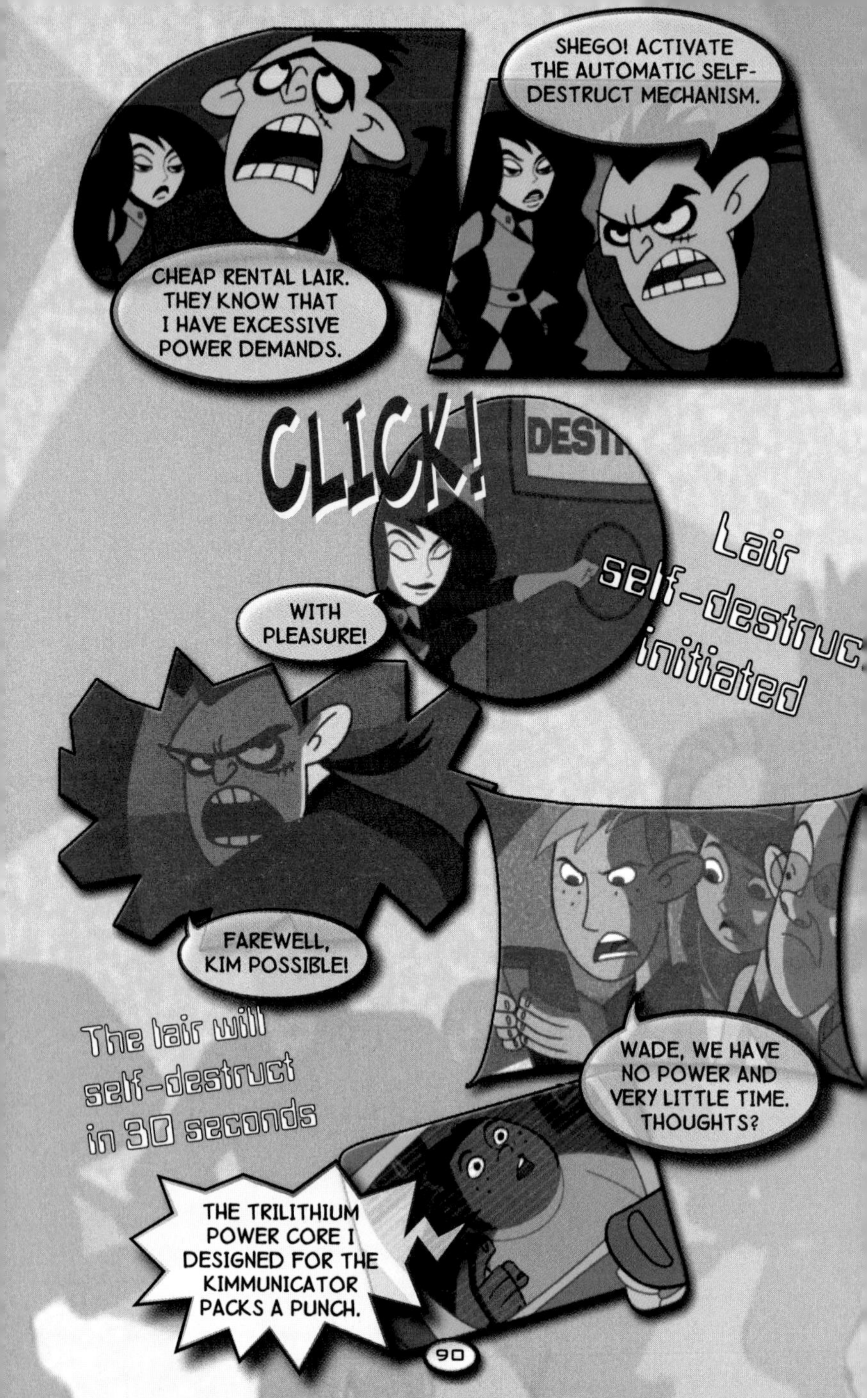
CHEAP RENTAL LAIR. THEY KNOW THAT I HAVE EXCESSIVE POWER DEMANDS.
SHEGO! ACTIVATE THE AUTOMATIC SELF-DESTRUCT MECHANISM.
CLICK!
DEST
WITH PLEASURE!
Lair self-destruc initiated
FAREWELL, KIM POSSIBLE!
The lair will self-destruct in 30 seconds
WADE, WE HAVE NO POWER AND VERY LITTLE TIME. THOUGHTS?
THE TRILITHIUM POWER CORE I DESIGNED FOR THE KIMMUNICATOR PACKS A PUNCH.

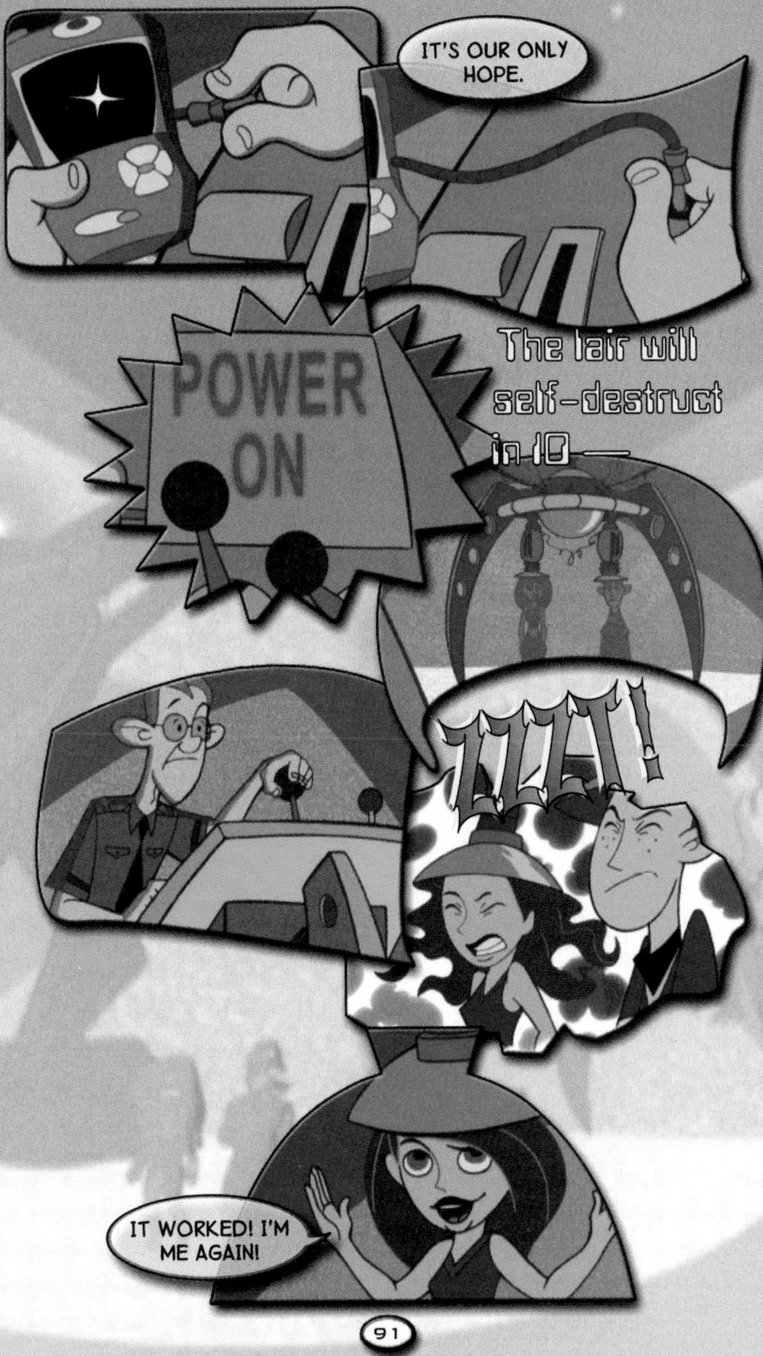
IT'S OUR ONLY HOPE.
POWER ON
The lair will self-destruct in 10 —
ZZAT!
IT WORKED! I'M ME AGAIN!

IT'S OUR ONLY HOPE.
POWER ON
The lair will self-destruct in 10—
ZZAT!
IT WORKED! I'M ME AGAIN!

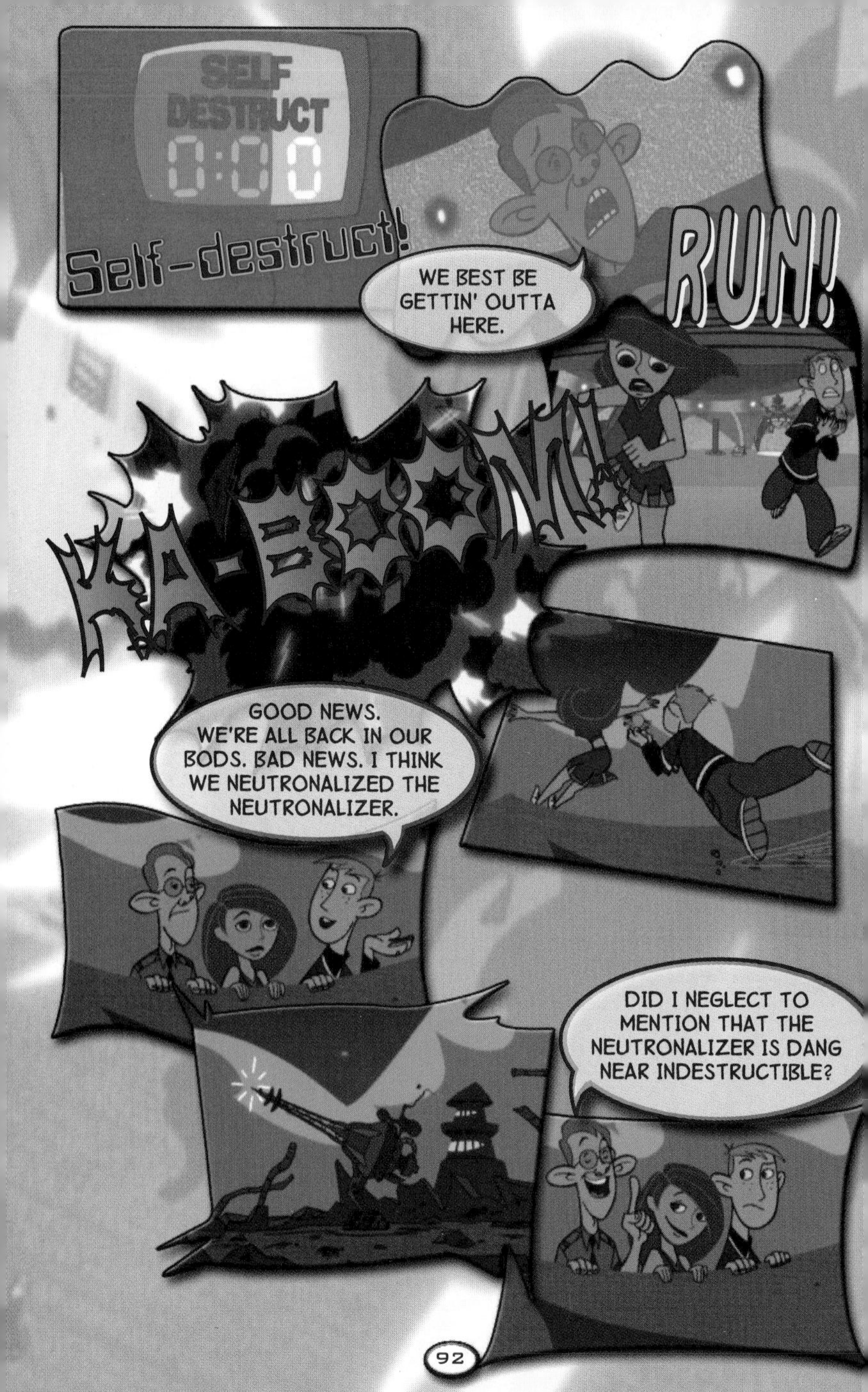

SELF DESTRUCT
0:00
Self-destruct!
WE BEST BE GETTIN' OUTTA HERE.
RUN!
KA-BOOM!
GOOD NEWS. WE'RE ALL BACK IN OUR BODS. BAD NEWS. I THINK WE NEUTRONALIZED THE NEUTRONALIZER.
DID I NEGLECT TO MENTION THAT THE NEUTRONALIZER IS DANG NEAR INDESTRUCTIBLE?

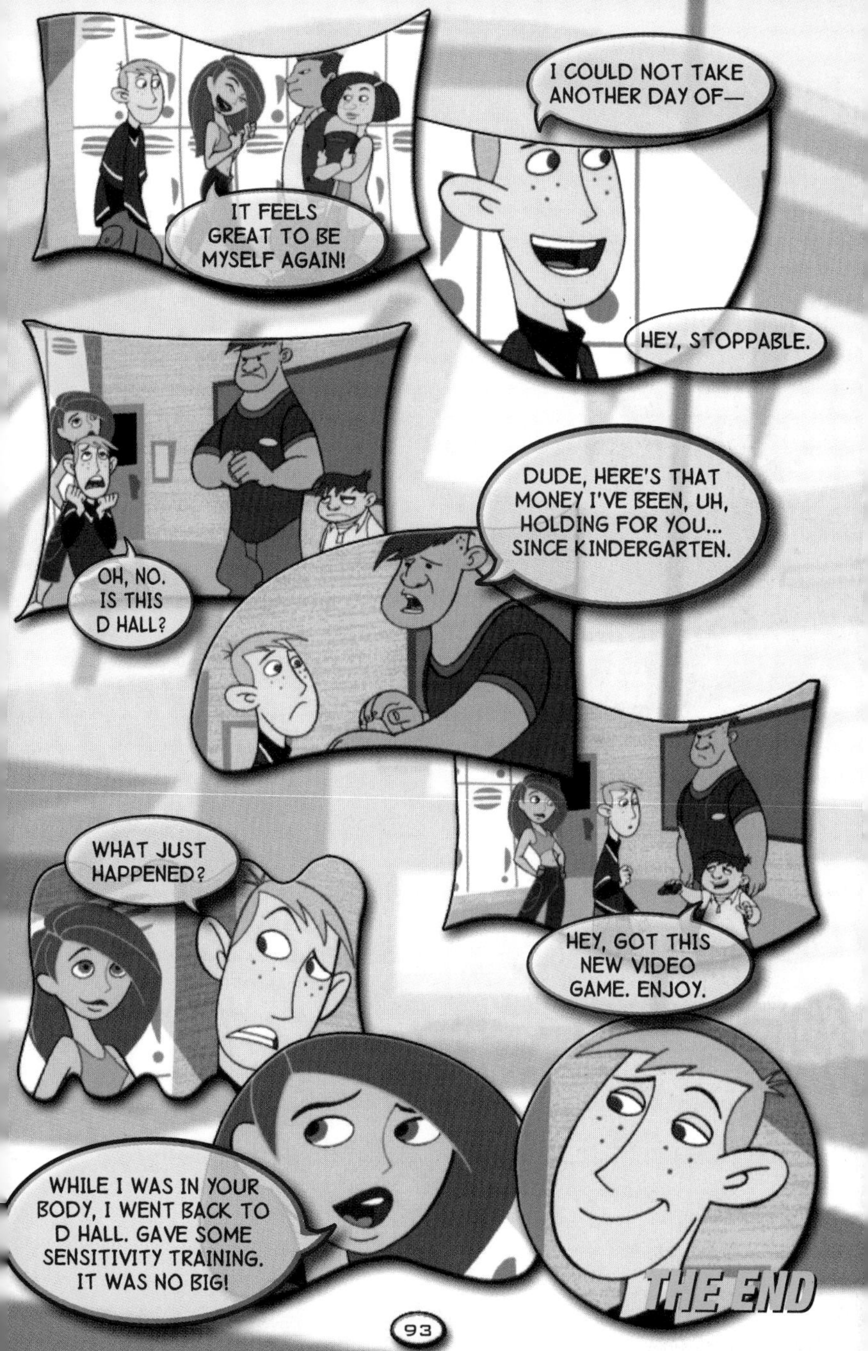
IT FEELS GREAT TO BE MYSELF AGAIN!
I COULD NOT TAKE ANOTHER DAY OF—
HEY, STOPPABLE.
OH, NO. IS THIS D HALL?
DUDE, HERE'S THAT MONEY I'VE BEEN, UH, HOLDING FOR YOU... SINCE KINDERGARTEN.
HEY, GOT THIS NEW VIDEO GAME. ENJOY.
WHAT JUST HAPPENED?
WHILE I WAS IN YOUR BODY, I WENT BACK TO D HALL. GAVE SOME SENSITIVITY TRAINING. IT WAS NO BIG!
THE END

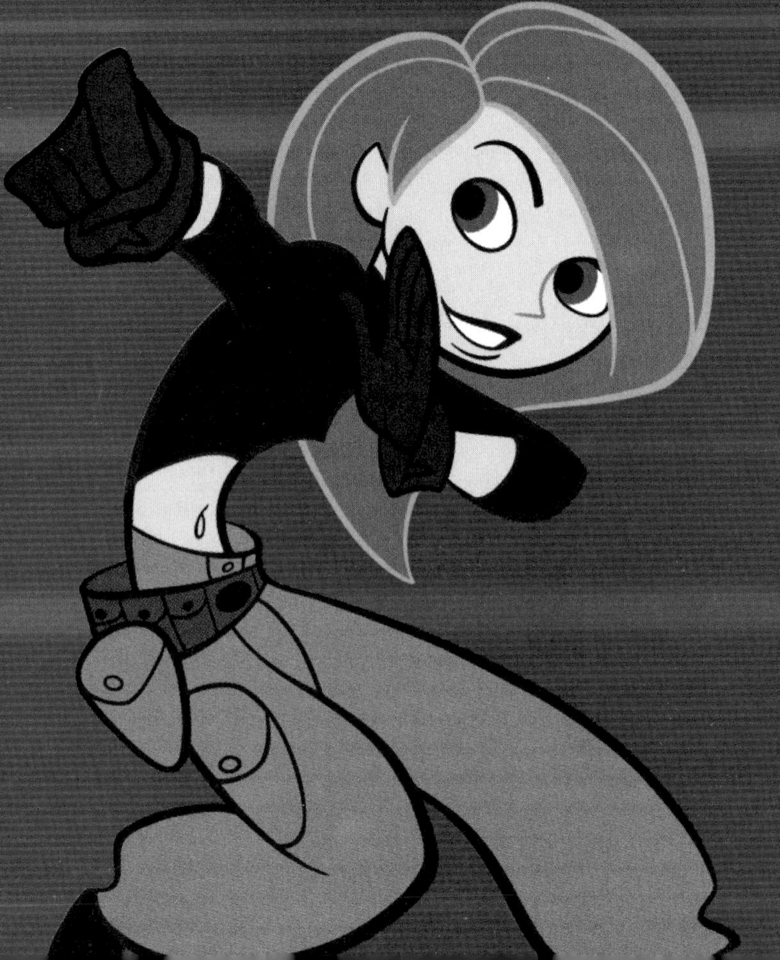